Leading Ethically in Schools and Other Organizations

Other Books By the Authors

Leading Through the Quagmire: Ethical Foundations, Critical Methods, and Practical Applications for School Leadership

Leading Ethically in Schools and Other Organizations

Inquiry, Case Studies, and Decision-Making

Bruce H. Kramer and
Ernestine K. Enomoto

With Deborah DeMeester
and Sharon Radd

ROWMAN & LITTLEFIELD
Lanham • Boulder • New York • London

Published by Rowman & Littlefield
A wholly owned subsidiary of The Rowman & Littlefield Publishing Group, Inc.
4501 Forbes Boulevard, Suite 200, Lanham, Maryland 20706
www.rowman.com

16 Carlisle Street, London W1D 3BT, United Kingdom

British Library Cataloguing in Publication Information Available

Library of Congress Cataloging-in-Publication Data

Kramer, Bruce H., 1956–
Leading ethically in schools and other organizations : inquiry, case studies, and decision-making / Bruce H. Kramer and Ernestine K. Enomoto.
pages cm.
Includes bibliographical references and index.
Revision of: Enomoto, Ernestine. Leading through the quagmire, 2007.
ISBN 978-1-4758-0637-3 (cloth : alk. paper) — ISBN 978-1-4758-0638-0 (pbk. : alk. paper) — ISBN 978-1-4758-0639-7 (ebook)
1. Educational leadership—Moral and ethical aspects—United States. 2. School administrators—Professional ethics—United States. 3. Leadership—Moral and ethical aspects—United States. I. Enomoto, Ernestine, 1949– II. Enomoto, Ernestine, 1949– Leading through the quagmire. III. Title.
LB1779.K736 2014
371.2—dc23
2014014472

∞ ™ The paper used in this publication meets the minimum requirements of American National Standard for Information Sciences Permanence of Paper for Printed Library Materials, ANSI/NISO Z39.48-1992.

Printed in the United States of America

Contents

Acknowledgments

Our partnership began with a mutual interest in teaching ethics and in the challenge of adequately conveying how to engage in ethical deliberation. The idea for writing this book occurred as we proposed how we might work with our students. Bringing our different yet complementary ideas together, we were able to build on a proposal for inquiry and for ultimately democratic ethics in leadership.

We thank Tom Koerner for believing that this would be a worthwhile endeavor. Special thanks go to Deb DeMeester and Sharon Radd, our collaborators in this revised edition, whose contributions have advanced the work tremendously. In addition, Deb provided the original artwork that graced the cover. Thank you to the many students who have offered thoughtful critiques, as well as added narratives, especially Magdeline Aagard, Wanelle Kaneshiro-Erdmann, Lauren Mark, Chris Milbrath, William F. Miller, and Riki Mitsunaga.

We extend our appreciation to university colleagues Carolyn Carr, Sharon Conley, Seongah Im, Don LaMagdeleine, Bob Paull, Katherine Ratliffe, Mitchell Ratner, Jerry Starratt, Tracy Trevorrow, and Lois Yamauchi for their encouragement and support in the writing process. Their thoughtful comments have encouraged our efforts all along the way. Many thanks to Jeanine DeGriselles for serving as Bruce's hands in the revision process.

Finally, we would like to thank our families for their unwavering commitment to us individually. We thank Misao Enomoto and Evelyn Emerson for being there for us always.

Foreword

I read this second edition of the book wearing several hats, and I suggest it would be an important book for any audience wearing one or another of these hats. First and foremost it will be useful for any professor who is teaching, or planning to teach, a course in ethics for aspiring or actual educational administrators. I also found it helpful for my own scholarly development as a scholar who writes about ethical leadership. As a professor in a school of education, I encounter practitioners in the field who are dealing with multiple ethical issues embedded in their daily practice and am asked to help them work through some of the stickier ones, and from that perspective, this book is also helpful.

Though I do not wear the hat of superintendent of schools, I would suggest that this book would be useful for that audience of educators to refresh their own ethical understanding and practice but also as a potentially useful book to discuss, chapter by chapter, over a series of monthly seminars with their principals. This exercise would be especially helpful since the authors argue, rightfully, that dealing with ethical issues requires a consistent method that in turn should be learned by everyone in the system, all the way down to the students themselves.

This second edition of the book further distinguishes itself from other books on the topic of ethical leadership. Though initially focused primarily within the practice of educational leadership, this second edition still provides a strong foundational introduction to ethical analysis and decision making for educators but is more expressly inclusive of ethical perspectives for leaders in other institutional settings such as law enforcement, corporate human resource administration, nonprofit organizations, and government service. This is especially helpful in university degree programs for preparing leaders of a variety of institutional settings who might all be taking the same course in ethical leadership.

I would also highlight the following excellent features of this second edition:

- It rather courageously includes a topic ignored, or poorly treated in some texts, namely, the connection between religious beliefs and ethics.
- It provides a generous treatment of feminist ethics that not only aids understanding of that important social development but also

blends that perspective into and enriches its method for addressing ethical issues facing administrators.

- It clearly posits the democratic social context as the diverse yet pragmatic source of values for ethical decision making.
- It provides a clear method for ethical decision making that goes beyond rationalistic, either–or, computational decision making to bring in
  - the desires and ideals of the people involved;
  - a search for a common enough good to get people to compromise; and
  - expectations of an imperfect and temporary decision that, while a genuine response to the immediate problem, is understood as a moment in a developing history of these specific people facing these specific circumstances who tomorrow will probably adjust and refashion another temporary advance.

- It provides two chapters with case studies fraught with ethical issues that enable readers to apply the analytical methods for ethical deliberations. Each case presentation is followed by guiding questions that relate to perspectives discussed in earlier chapters, thus providing a helpful scaffolding for delving into the case and practicing one's ethical deliberations.

This is a book by two professors who have mastered their pedagogy and the design of learning experiences for their courses. They teach in different contexts—one in a Catholic university, the other in a state university. They use differing pedagogies—one more socratically provocative, the other more of a stage director who coaxes out student self-understanding and cognitive clarification through debate and role-playing. One is a male, the other a female. These differences can appeal to a broad audience who can find in the range of the authors' dissimilarities possibilities for crafting their own pedagogy.

The authors share, however, a strong commitment to a democratic leadership approach to creating a community of ethical decision makers who teach one another in the process of using a common method for ethical deliberation. That method is exploratory (attempting to describe fully what is actually at stake); dynamic (the method is not a one-dimensional sequence of logical deductions but rather flows with the evolving process of constructing, deconstructing, and reconstructing a rich understanding of the situation); imaginative (besides exploring the duties called into play, it involves imagining various responses that might improve the whole context of the problem); and capacity building (the use of a consistent reflective inquiry method strengthens participants' capacity for moral deliberation and moral action). I will leave it to the reader to discover the power of this method. Let me only say that I find this method the most helpful one I have seen in the various treatments of ethical decision making in the recent literature on the topic.

The core strength of this book, I believe, is its balance. The authors provide a clear presentation of foundational theories and show how each perspective can be used to counterbalance the exclusive use of one perspective. This generous-enough treatment of the more traditional approaches is brought into dialogue with more critical theories, especially through a refreshing exposition of feminist ethics.

The authors then go on to frame the whole ethical context and a sophisticated method for responding to ethical dilemmas through an updated version of Dewey's democratic landscape in dialogue with ecofeminism's sensitivity to the social ecology of ethical challenges. This balance throughout the book does not result in bland, watered-downed generalities but rather in a deeper and stronger leadership approach to ethical decision making that is clearly in line with much of the best literature on distributed leadership. I believe that this volume will become one of the most helpful books available for courses in ethical leadership in administrative preparation programs.

Robert J. Starratt
Emeritus Professor, Boston College

Introduction

It may not seem like much of a problem. The district policy clearly states that possession of any weapon or weapon-like toy on the school premises is an automatic expulsion. The school board and superintendent support the policy 100 percent. So why does the principal, Kareen Escoban, feel so torn by what has happened? Rosa, a student in her school, was found carrying a small toy gun in her backpack.

Not a gun-toting youngster, she is a six-year-old kindergartner who recently emigrated from Mexico. She does not speak much English, and Kareen suspects neither do her parents. The plastic toy gun was a prize won at the neighborhood store. Did Rosa even know it was a "weapon-like toy"? The principal feels caught between her duty to uphold the policy and her desire to consider the circumstances of the situation. To this day, Kareen wonders whether she did the right thing for both Rosa and the school.

Or consider Brad Ng, a first-year police officer in a midsized metropolitan area, who is faced with an immediate dilemma between his police academy training and the methods his mentor/partner uses when confronting situations in communities of color. Brad is the first Asian officer on the force. He needs to be accepted by the other officers but finds himself told to sign off on questionable reports. His partner seems to be pushing the "blue line" that delineates the culture of policing, or is he actually testing whether Brad will remain loyal to his fellow officers? What's the right thing to do?

These incidents happen, as do so many similar kinds of incidents in classrooms, school yards, businesses, and communities across the country. Leaders are called upon to make judgments where sometimes the rules don't seem to take into account the finer points of the situation. As a Latina like Rosa, Kareen is pulled by the circumstances of the kindergartner's case, understanding how language and cultural differences are often at odds with the school. But as the elementary school principal, Kareen has a duty to obey the rules and protect all those who are in her care.

Brad is excited to become a police officer and achieve his dreams. However, this case immediately tests his loyalties, so much so that it is compromising his health. Here are ethical situations that would test the judgment of the most seasoned professional, the stuff of what true leadership is about.

Negotiating situations like Kareen's and Brad's is what this book is about. It is about recognizing that ethical tensions arise from perceptions of one's duty, considering "best" outcomes along with important personal and professional values. All this relates to one's social class, race–ethnicity, gender, religion, and culture while considering shared societal values and beliefs. It is also about critiquing individual experiences and challenging habitual responses that fail to address the situation at hand. These are aspects of becoming democratic leaders who must make ethical decisions in increasingly diversified settings.

ASSUMPTIONS OF THIS BOOK

If ethics are central to school leadership, then three assumptions need to be stated up front. First, we use philosopher William Frankena's (1963) definition of ethics, that which is intended to be helpful in answering questions about what is right, good, or obligatory. Ethical judgments can be about a specific situation, for example, "What is to be done about Rosa's case?" Or the decision can be general, for instance, "How can we ensure all students are granted an equal opportunity for advancement in our society?"

As school leaders, we would likely make judgments about what we should do as well as what others might do, what is deemed just or caring action, what should be tolerated, and so on. Additionally, we want to be able to analyze and critique our reasoning and judgments. This is called meta-ethical thinking, which examines the meaning of our actions and reasoning for them.

Second, we assume that all decisions, regardless how small, have an ethical component. Even the simple administrative task of assigning lockers or establishing a master schedule can pose ethical dilemmas for educators. These decisions are judgments to be rendered based upon personal, professional, and communal values and beliefs. There will be intended and unintended consequences of our actions whether it be with colleagues, employees, the people we serve, or the community at large. For these reasons, all decisions, whether consciously or unconsciously made, can be interpreted as applied ethics.

Third, we assume that within our role as leaders is caring for the needs of everyone within our sphere of influence. That is, leadership must serve everyone fairly, equitably, and respectfully while negotiating the diverse needs and different options available. In schools, leaders might consider such things as how educators might ensure consistent high-quality teaching and learning for all students, how schools can provide for those with greater needs, and how to balance the demands made by varied constituencies. For those who lead, the challenge includes understanding one's context as well as one's personal and professional values.

Proceeding on these three assumptions, we consider how leaders might make ethical judgments about individual needs as well as those of the group. How do leaders act ethically for their institutions or the system as a whole?

To answer this question, John Dewey suggested that democracy might be an appropriate meta-ethic to respond with as well as to critique our actions. We introduce an inquiry method to guide ethical deliberation and conflict resolution. Such a method allows for understanding the current context of schools and other organizations along with the habitual responses that might stymie action. It also calls for more creative problem solving, followed by reflective discernment once action has been taken. We propose that working ethical situations using this inquiry method will create a more responsive and caring place, no matter the context.

WHAT GUIDES OUR WRITING

Our intent in this book is to provide a combination of philosophical grounding and practical application using a democratic approach to ethical deliberation and decision making. We are not prescribing the exact outcomes or right processes in your specific case because we believe that leadership is contextual. That is, it must account for the particular individuals, issues, and challenges of the given situation so that a one-size-fits-all solution probably will not suffice. But we do offer a set of guidelines to direct your thinking in the particular situation.

One of these guidelines was discussed earlier—the idea that democratic leadership is fundamental to do the work required of school leaders, indeed all leaders. A democratic approach will strive to honor individual differences and be inclusive of the multiplicity of perspectives held. At the same time, it will consider the good of all. It will attempt to address the demands of diverse individuals while under the constraints of uniformity and standards-based education. We hope to demonstrate how a democratic approach to leadership can be a workable model for resolving conflicts and negotiating the tough ethical decisions that leaders must make.

Another guideline that informs this book is that inquiry and reflection are critical in decision making. In making sound ethical judgments, leaders need to investigate problems fully and comprehensively. As much as possible, we believe that they need to be open to information from all sources, communicating with the parties involved in the situation. They need to be able to reflect thoughtfully on intended actions and consequences. We propose a method that will support doing the necessary inquiry and reflection demanded of those in leadership positions.

A third guideline is the idea of "working the situation" rather than resolving it. To paraphrase Dewey, resolving a situation does not mean that disparate viewpoints do not exist. Tensions between individuals will remain, waxing and waning as time progresses and as the situation evolves. The idea of working the situation is preferable because it allows leaders to see the larger whole, one that cannot be totally controlled.

Peter Vaill (1996) likened leading to being in permanent white water going down river rapids. We are not in control, but we can learn to control our own responses and reflect upon actions to be taken. This metaphor views leadership as the raft that will get us through the rapids. We see leaders ensuring that ethical deliberation and judgment take place in institutions. Further, we believe that democratic leadership must be in the context of a moral imperative for service.

MORAL IMPERATIVE FOR LEADERSHIP

Michael Fullan (2003) described the moral imperative for schools as "having a system where all students learn, the gap between high and low performance becomes greatly reduced, and what people learn enables them to be successful citizens and workers in a morally-based knowledge society" (p. 29). It is not sufficient that a school administrator manages competently, maintains good public relations, and sustains high student achievement. More is demanded of the leadership.

"At the school level . . . the moral imperative of the principal involves leading deep cultural change that mobilizes the passion and commitment of teachers, parents, and others to improve the learning of all students, including closing the achievement gap" (Fullan, 2003, p. 41).

This means looking beyond the technical and managerial solutions toward one's responsibilities to others as well as to school (Sergiovanni, 1992, 1995). For example, administrators can create specific conditions to address diverse student needs and care for their families (Beck, 1994; Noddings, 2003). They can encourage inclusive teaching and learning as well as explore how culturally relevant teaching practices can be enacted (Riehl, 2000).

But more than considering strategies to deliver outcomes, administrators can engage with others in the work of schooling. They need to take responsibility for delivering authentic learning and relevant practices that build citizens for a democracy (Starratt, 2004). It is this work that designates school leaders to be "moral agents," different from those of other institutions (Greenfield, 1993).

The moral imperative for education extends beyond the school. According to Fullan (2003), leaders at regional and national levels need to be encouraged to help each other and work collaboratively as in "a culture of shared commitment across the district" (p. 52). Consider what it might be like for a principal whose school is placed on the watch list to have all administrators in the district offer to give support and assistance. Rather than go it alone, that principal would be able to tap into the shared commitment of the entire district.

Riehl (2000) also suggested that school administrators build school community connections that extend into local communities. Schools can be mobilized into the process of community development and provide services to strengthen communities (Strike, 2006). Here is a much broader vision of what moral imperative might be beyond schools and districts with implications for the future.

While our frame of reference is of education, we have robust experience working with nearly every other profession. The moral imperatives described above, both institutional and contextual as applied to schools, can also apply to other community institutions. Businesses, government, civil service, philanthropic organizations, and other community institutions have their own moral imperatives. Each leader serving in them has a responsibility within her or his professional communities, associations, and networks. Even the largest corporations recognize that ignoring the moral imperative of responsibility to their communities is done at their own peril.

LEADERSHIP PREPARATION

In preparing prospective leaders for their work, university faculties have stipulated that an examination of moral–ethical issues be included among course offerings. This contrasts with earlier administrative preparation programs of the 1970s according to McCarthy (1999), who reviewed University Council of Educational Administration (UCEA) programs. She found that little attention was given to ethical issues in earlier programs, whereas by the 1990s, ethical issues and concerns had been either incorporated within traditional course offerings or delivered in special seminars.

In the past decade, evidence suggests that more attention has been placed on issues of values and ethics, with more integration of the topic within coursework. Shapiro and Stefkovich (2005) indicated a broader perspective than one grounded primarily in the justice perspective (Strike, Haller, & Soltis, 1998). Other approaches include perspectives that embrace caring (Beck, 1994; Noddings, 2003), critique (Starratt, 2003), and a combination of both (Enomoto, 1997; Katz, Noddings, & Strike, 1999; Starratt, 2003).

STANDARDS AND ETHICS

Standards for moral leadership have given further impetus to the study of ethics in leadership preparation. In November 1996, the Interstate School Leaders Licensure Consortium (ISLLC) specified six national performance standards in school administrator preparation, identifying the knowledge, skills, and dispositions deemed necessary to be effective educational leaders (ISLLC, 1996). The Council of Chief State School Officers, representing state superintendents nationwide, adopted the ISLLC standards and encouraged other professional educational associations and agencies to do the same. The council also encouraged that similar standards be adopted by educational agencies and regulatory bodies within each state.

According to Maxcy (2002), the ISLLC standards have been most influential in moving educational administration toward a standards-based model for administrator preparation. Reflective of the diversification of American society, a standard on social justice was added in 2008 (NPBEA, 2011).

Of the ISLLC standards, Standard Five relates specifically to ethics and leadership necessary to ensure the success of all students. In achieving this standard, a prospective school leader is expected to know and understand various ethical frameworks and professional codes of ethics in order to serve diverse school communities. Also important is knowledge of the values of one's specific community coupled with an understanding of the diverse views held by its members.

Within the national context, ISLLC Standard Five stipulates that an administrator be responsible for upholding the rights and beliefs of our country. It is expected that our school administrators understand and commit to providing for the common good while ensuring that every student receives a free, quality education.

In 2011, the ISLLC standards were revised by the National Policy Board for Education Administration (NPBEA). These standards were crafted with an informing framework of student accountability and performance indicators.

The revised Standard Five is as follows:

> A school-level education leader applies knowledge that promotes the success of every student by acting with integrity, fairness, and in an ethical manner to ensure a school system of accountability for every student's academic and social success by modeling school principles of self-awareness, reflective practice, transparency, and ethical behavior as related to their roles within the school; safeguarding the values of democracy, equity, and diversity within the school; evaluating the potential moral and legal consequences of decision making in the school; and promoting social justice within the school to ensure individual student needs inform all aspects of schooling (NPBEA, 2011, p. 18).

Given the new direction of these leadership standards of ethics, and more course offerings addressing ethical issues, there is a clear need for prospective administrators to understand ethical concerns in their decision making, particularly in balancing the needs of an accountability system with the promotion of democracy and social justice. How to do so in resolving ethical situations is what we present in this book.

OVERVIEW OF THIS BOOK

The three main sections of the book are Part I: Ethical Foundations (chapters 1–5), Part II: Methods (chapters 6–7), and Part III: Applications (chapters 8–10).

Part I: Ethical Foundations

The five chapters in this section provide a philosophical and conceptual grounding for thinking about moral–ethical leadership, democratic education, and inquiry-based methods.

In chapter 1, we consider how school leaders make decisions. Determining the bus schedule or filling a teacher vacancy might be done in the same way year after year. But each decision calls into question the administrator's choice and reasoning. How do leaders examine their decisions, acknowledge habitual choices, and make conscious decisions? We draw from Greek philosophers shaping our Western ethical thinking and the kinds of questions that we might ask in deciding what is right. Consideration is given to personal as well as professional ideology in decision making. Further, we propose considering democratic ethics and its implications for school leadership.

Chapter 2 presents four common sources of ethical tension that create conflicts among individuals and groups. The first source, duty-based ethics, proposes ways to consider ethical conduct within one's personal and professional duties. Second, desires-based ethics (also known as ends or outcomes) focus on what is deemed best for the majority. The third source of ethical tension emphasizes the individual's character and behavior (virtue ethics); the fourth source is on the group or societal perspective of character and behavior.

Grounded in Western philosophical language, each source can form an ethical system with assumptions and beliefs used in decision making. Conflicts arise when people operate from different ethical systems, and we illustrate this in the chapter. Judgments and consequences are part of our deliberation. We specify what can inform our judgments as well as how we might weigh consequences for actions.

In chapter 3, we explore religion and ethical decision making. While it is often difficult to discuss, we propose the need to address how our religious backgrounds might influence our ethical deliberation and decisions. Beginning with a definition of religion, we consider how religious thinking has evolved and varied over time given the religious freedoms practiced in American society. Dewey's distinction between religion and religious attitude enables us to be more open to inquiry. We consider the work expected of leaders choosing to honor religious freedom while accommodating diversity and multiple perspectives.

Extending the critique on predominant ways of thinking, chapter 4 on feminist ethics offers an alternative perspective that informs our moral–ethical decisions different from an ethic of justice and moral development. We take an in-depth look at feminist ethics, defining feminism and suggesting how it applies to ethical decision making as school administrators. With its limitations in mind, we close the chapter by suggesting how ecofeminism offers us a model of critique that is highly appropriate to democratic leadership.

Chapter 5 is new to this edition. Acknowledging the social reality of increasing diversity in American society and advocating against the inequities among different groups, we describe the work of social justice leadership and offer three theoretical lenses of that agenda. Moving toward a pragmatic approach to ethical decision making, we suggest some internal barriers and offer considerations to skillfully negotiate complex social issues in educational and other public settings.

Part II: Methods

In these two chapters, we specify a rationale and means to engage in ethical deliberation in a systematic way. In chapter 6, we present Dewey's ethic of democratic leadership as an effective means in engaging others and striving toward collaboration. We consider how leaders traditionally look at their work in contrast with how they might ethically view their roles and responsibilities. Dewey wrote:

> [Traditional leadership roles] encourage the idea that some "leader" is to show the way; others are to follow in imitation. It takes time to arouse minds from apathy and lethargy, to get them thinking for themselves, to share in making plans, to take part in their execution. But without active cooperation both in forming aims and in carrying them out there is no possibility of a common good. (Dewey & Tufts, 1932b, p. 347)

Thus, we propose an inquiry method that aims to be inclusive, contextual, democratic, and empirical. It asks leaders to subsume their individual desires and take others into account. We illustrate using an example of an administrator struggling with an ethical dilemma. Working through the example, we show how inquiry and facilitation might work but present a fuller description of the method in the next chapter.

Chapter 7 details the inquiry approach for working through tough ethical problems to arrive at decisions. It takes the reader sequentially through four phases of discernment and action. We also suggest collaborative decision making that can apply to public settings whereby many members need to be informed and make decisions collectively. Just as health care professionals consult ethics boards in reflecting about dilemmas, so too might schools and school systems consider how public discourse can be incorporated whereby ethical choices may be debated, exposed, examined, and enacted. Such collaborative inquiry and dialogue fulfill the democratic charge.

Part III: Applications

Chapter 8 presents specific education cases for ethical deliberation and decision making in K–12 and higher education settings, and chapter 9 presents cases in other leadership contexts. The reader may wish to select cases that are of particular interest. Each case is presented first in synopsis and then in greater detail. The case narrative identifies a problem or situation, reveals the participants' thinking, raises some key issues, and suggests possible implications. A general set of discussion questions applies the inquiry method, and more specific questions relate to the individual cases.

While some cases are event specific, all suggest historical context that encourages the reader to dig deeper and probe more rigorously. Unlike case narratives that present problems and offer solutions, the reader is invited to consider personal as well as professional reactions and alternatives to the dilemmas. Our experience is that ethical cases require working through an iterative process that will evolve as one's knowledge and skills increase.

Chapter 10 discusses teaching ethics. Beginning with our own experiences, we describe how we have approached teaching ethics, using the inquiry method. We also share our commonalities and differences in struggling to make sense of philosophical language in ways relevant to our students. Beyond the teaching of ethics in leadership preparation, we suggest that democratic ethics can be applied to the classroom and beyond. We extend this to the role of leader as teacher and specify how democratic ethics as a framework propose a different style of leadership.

CONCLUSION

As authors, we first developed our friendship around the challenges experienced in teaching ethics to prospective leaders. What ethical foundations would be beneficial yet not overwhelming? How could ethics be made relevant and meaningful? What examples illustrate concepts such as utilitarianism? What is meant by ethical deliberation? We have also found that students struggle with personal as well as professional decisions. They wonder about whether their decisions are ethically sound. They reflect that doing what is right and good might not be enough in dealing with diverse views and conflicting needs.

We wrote this book for students, practitioner friends, and the many Kareen Escoban and Brad Ngs who work in schools, businesses, and communities. It is our attempt to use ethical language and logic to discuss what is the right thing to do. It is also about remaining open and inclusive as democratic practitioners leading diverse institutions. By reading this book, we hope that you will gain a better understanding of how to think through ethical dilemmas and work toward resolving them well.

I

Ethical Foundations

ONE

Ethical Foundations

Leadership is about judgment, and that implies moral consideration. Basically, leaders must ask, "What is the right thing to do?" and "What good will result?" There is nothing more basic to leadership than the judgments implied in these two questions. By asking questions and reflecting upon the answers, leaders accrue the knowledge needed to provide the direction required to achieve the vision, mission, and goals of their organizations. In this chapter we provide basic concepts and tenets used in ethical judgment and democratic leadership.

We begin the chapter by setting the context of Western ethical thinking and describing its Greek origins. Next, we discuss how individual and group needs may be more difficult to reconcile in ways that work for all. Third, we look specifically at the concepts of *right actions* and *good ends*, describing what is meant in terms of ethical decision making. Specifically we consider antecedent and consequential factors that determine right and good. Finally, we explore the concept of an ethical dilemma and relate it to leadership. All these basic concepts lay the foundation for discussing moral leadership and democratic ethics.

GREEK ORIGINS

Ethics as characterized by Western ethical philosophy can be described as "the search for a rational understanding of the principles of human conduct" (Rowe, 1991, p. 121). What is meant by a good life? What is a good person or a good society? How do we know what is right? What is considered to be virtuous? These questions have dominated Western thinking, beginning with the ancient Greeks to the present day. While contemporary issues and perspectives may differ somewhat, this line of thinking is still recognizable as descendent from discussions and debate that took place in Greek city-states of the fifth and fourth centuries BCE.

Probably the most influential Greek philosophers from that period were Socrates, Plato, and Aristotle. Socrates (ca. 469–399 BCE), nicknamed the Gadfly, was said to sting people into thinking clearly for themselves by asking probing questions that critiqued the Athenian way of life and its established social order. He was so critical of society that he was put on trial and later killed for his views. But his aim was to raise people's awareness to a higher level, reflecting justice for all, including the least of society's members.

After Socrates, the term *ethics* (in Greek, *ethos* or *ethike*) came to mean "questioning of the sacred customs" (Fasching, deChant, & Lantigua, 2011, p. 14). A guiding tenet of his philosophy was that "a position is only as good as the arguments that support it." He cautioned against taking any proposition whatsoever as authoritative and criticized social customs and norms.

Despite this strong orientation toward criticism, Socrates held a functional view that all humans have ultimate purpose (in Greek, *telos*) and that they need to determine what that purpose is. Accordingly, virtue (*arête*) was derived from this purposeful wisdom. Once their purpose was known, humans could reason and would always know what was the right thing to do. Socrates was confident that if anyone did wrong, he or she had not thought enough about the matter. His belief in human reasoning was captured in the maxim "No one goes wrong deliberately."

Socrates's student Plato (ca. 427–347 BCE) wrote dialogues from his teacher and later developed his own ideas about the individual, the state, and morality differing from but extending Socratic tradition. One notion was that empirical knowledge (sensory perception) was filtered through human reasoning. Plato proposed that real knowledge, by contrast, was structured in the universe and unchanging. Mankind would need to "penetrate beyond the veil of appearances to the hidden, unchanging reality" in understanding the knowledge of goodness (Buckle, 1991, p. 162). For Plato, real knowledge was morality.

Aristotle (ca. 384–322 BCE) was Plato's student and later became the tutor of Alexander the Great. Agreeing with Plato that human beings were "essentially social beings," Aristotle was more pragmatic and interested in "what ordinary people thought about morality on a day-to-day basis" (Robinson & Garratt, 2004, p. 40).

In writing the *Nicomachean Ethics*, Aristotle provided a rational basis for the idea of goodness and justice that occurs from organizing a society in a harmonious way. There was legal justice, which man created, and natural justice, "which everywhere has the same force and does not exist by people thinking this or that" (*Nichomachean Ethics*, vol. 7, as quoted in Buckle, 1991, p. 162).

Despite various critiques over time, the Greek philosophy introduced by Socrates and developed by Plato and Aristotle remains a cornerstone of our Western ethical reasoning. Like those philosophers, we identify with the importance of human reasoning, the freedom to choose our individual actions, and the belief that it is possible to live peacefully with others.

According to Rowe (1991), "The rise of Greek ethics can be seen in large part as a reflection of the overlaying of a fundamentally individual-istic ethos with the demands for co-operative behavior implied by the political institutions of the city-state" (p. 127). These Greek philosophers believed that ultimately there was no conflict between the individual and the state. Moreover, they held to a belief that by using reason and engaging in argument and debate, we could arrive at knowing the right action to take.

THE INDIVIDUAL AND SOCIETY

As early as the fourth century CE, St. Augustine of Hippo (354–430) linked the Christian Gospel teachings with Plato's philosophy. He believed that with Adam's fall from Eden, all people had an evil impulse and needed to be restrained by the power of the state and the laws of the church (Thompson, 2003). Augustine's *Confessions* reflected an individual's inner turmoil and struggles wrestling with God. But there was clearly a separate realm for the religious (the city of God ruled by the church and its bishops) different from the secular (the city of man ruled by kings and emperors) (Fasching, deChant, & Lantigua, 2011).

By the medieval period, St. Thomas Aquinas (1224–1274) argued for societal laws to be for the good of all and reflective of "natural law," which was God's providential ordering of the world (Thompson, 2003). Individuals needed to be tempered and subjected by reason, governance, and divine rule. Aquinas declared,

> The human will is subject to three orders. Firstly, to the order of its own reason, secondly to the others of human government, be it spiritual or temporal, and thirdly, it is subject to the universal order of Divine rule. (*Summa Theologiae, Ia, Iiae, q8, aI* as quoted in Haldane, 1991, p. 133)

What he and other Christian theologians added to Greek philosophy was divine intervention and transformation of virtues into God's blessings.

In the fourteenth century, Western Europe was transformed by the rise of empirical science, the fragmentation of the Church of Rome, and the beginnings of the Protestant Reformation. Attempting to retain ground, Catholic scholars continued to expound on the works of Aquinas and Aristotle as exemplified by the Dominicans, who advanced the argument for the legitimate use of violence to defend society. More aligned with the times was a return to Platonic doctrines, promoting humanity and its moral value. This philosophy was later embodied in Renaissance humanism, which by the fifteenth and sixteenth centuries emphasized human accomplishments over God's role in them.

Since individuals needed to determine a right course of action, a study of ethics emerged. Some thinkers believed that ethics was man's egoistic response to maximize good ends for himself while trying to live with others (Midgley, 1991). Thomas Hobbes (1588–1679), a seventeenth-century English philosopher, contended that human life was basically "solitary, poor, nasty, brutish and short." If humans were left to their own devices, there would be social anarchy.

Hobbes proposed that human beings needed to agree upon a "social contract" in order to be regulated and avoid conflicts with each other. "Everyone comes to agree to a legal agreement not to kill or steal from each other, because it's ultimately in everyone's interest" (Robinson & Garratt, 2004, p. 56). In humanism, the notion of a contractual agreement established by men in society placed them at the center of the moral universe, not God or the Divine.

Contrasting Hobbes's bleak view of mankind, Jean-Jacques Rousseau (1712–1778) espoused that humans were born as moral beings with the potential for goodness. Writing *Emile* about a young man's education, Rousseau proposed educating children toward their innate goodness and not allowing their innocence to be corrupted. His writings spurred the Romantic movement, a return to the natural order of life and living harmoniously within it. American philosopher Henry David Thoreau (1817–1862) expressed this philosophy in writing *Walden*, which espoused a simpler, more natural way of life.

By the end of the nineteenth century, the simple natural life in America was rapidly being replaced by increasing urbanization, industrialization, and waves of immigration. At this point in our history, we agreed to put aside some of our self-interest for a greater social good. This was a significant development because social groups were made up of individuals who often had specific desires and needs that were not always compatible or complementary with each other. Putting aside individual interests was deemed necessary if we were to live collectively, each surrendering something for the good of the whole. But how was this to be done?

Two different ethical philosophies emerged to answer this question. The first, utilitarianism, was introduced by English philosopher Jeremy Bentham (1748–1832). In *Principle of Utility*, he wrote that humans were either seeking out pleasure or avoiding pain, arguing that

> [i]nstead of relying on vague ideas about feelings or conscience, you classify and measure any action in terms of how many units of pain or pleasure it will produce. (Robinson & Garratt, 2004, p. 71)

To judge actions based upon results, Bentham introduced "the general good," referring to the greatest happiness of the greatest number. He theorized that in any situation with moral choices, "the right thing to do is that which is likely to produce the greatest happiness for the greatest number of people" (Thompson, 2003, p. 67).

Similarly, John Stuart Mill (1806–1873) favored utilitarianism but proposed that it be made less materialistic by prioritizing cultural and spiritual kinds of happiness rather than only physical and sensual pleasures. Further, he believed that "morality should still be about obeying moral rules, even if the rules were decided upon Utilitarian grounds" (Thompson, 2003, p. 76). In his essay *On Liberty*, Mill wrote that as long as people did not interfere with the freedoms of others, they should be allowed to think and do as they pleased.

Different from utilitarianism was the ethical proposition advanced by the Prussian philosopher Immanuel Kant (1724–1804). In *Fundamental Principles of the Metaphysics of Morals* (1785), he proposed that moral action is done out of a sense of duty rather than as a result of following one's inclinations or desires and that such action is executed without regard for the consequences. That is, individuals act out of a personal sense of what is right.

Given this duties-oriented, or *deontological*, stance, Kant believed that "ethics is all about what these duties are, how we find out what they are, and why we must obey them" (Thompson, 2003, p. 81). Using reasoning, we could work out what to do by a test of universality, that is to say, by asking what would happen if everyone did the same thing and there were no exceptions. This became Kant's system of compulsory rules, or the "categorical imperative." More will be said about this in chapter 2.

Kant also believed that ordinary people could learn to apply abstract moral principles. While earlier philosophers did not believe that everyone possessed a methodical way of consciously using such principles, Kant held that morality could actually be used by all (Schneewind, 1991). This view of moral autonomy, that individuals were capable of seeing for themselves and deciding for the good of all, held a major place in the nineteenth and early twentieth centuries.

Both ethical philosophies had their share of critics. G. W. F. Hegel (1770–1831) argued that Kant's formal principle came from the institutions, vocabularies, and orientations of one's society, not strictly an individual choice as Kant proposed (Schneewind, 1991). Likewise, Karl Marx (1818–1883) suggested that humans were products of their social class, deriving attitudes, values, and beliefs determined by an economic structure. He saw workers cut off from their labor and functioning in a process where others reaped the profits. Laborers were subject to their employers and employment and thus not morally autonomous.

Another critic, French existentialist Jean-Paul Sartre (1905–1980), believed in the uniqueness of each human being. This view of moral philosophy could not be derived from purpose (as Aristotle proposed), rationality (Kant), or pain versus pleasure (Bentham). For Sartre, morality was about the freedom to choose one's action. Drawing from Nietzsche, Sartre argued that "morality rested on nothing but the totally untrammeled free decision of each individual," and each must make a "purely personal decision about it—and then, to be in good faith, live accordingly" (Schneewind, 1991, p. 155).

Regardless of whether we believe, as Sartre did, that individuals are personally responsible or, as Marx and Hegel did, that social, political, and economic institutions dictate individual thinking and preempt morally autonomous action, the tensions between the individual and society continue to play out as we attempt to consider what is best for the majority (utilitarianism) and what duty might determine is the ethical thing to do (deontology).

RIGHT ACTION AND GOOD ENDS

In ethical language, the words *right* and *good* have specific meanings. *Right* refers to the process, way, or path of action. Its focus is on the means rather than the end. By contrast, the word *good* refers to the end result, product, or outcome of an action. This distinction should be retained in addressing ethical questions about what to do, why, and how to do so (Kramer, 2006b).

Throughout history, these two concepts have been defined and redefined within their historical and social contexts. For example, before the time of Socrates in fifth-century BCE Greece, good meant anything that the king was (e.g., wealthy and powerful) or did (e.g., conquered enemies, sired many children). Others could be wealthy or powerful, but since they were not the king, their good outcomes were not considered the same good as the king's. Later, the word *good* took on a more general meaning, not only whether things were associated with the king but rather how they affected other people.

Most leaders find themselves making decisions where they weigh what is good for individuals against what is good for the group as a whole. In the educational setting, consider classroom management. Teachers often judge how much behavioral disruption they will tolerate before acting to control it. They could ask "Is the class becoming too unruly? Does it serve to have this child who is misbehaving in with the whole class and participating with others?" As leaders of the class, teachers must weigh the good of the individual child against the good of the class as a whole.

Likewise, school leaders weigh individual needs with group needs in judging good outcomes. As a principal, you may have encountered assertive parents advocating very effectively for their children, and you may have been persuaded to agree. You might also recognize the need to look beyond individual needs of certain children, acknowledging that one person's needs, though well served, are met at the expense of other students in the school. Here, you are weighing the good for the many against the good for the one.

To further complicate matters, individual needs may be conflicting with groups whose interests are not necessarily aligned. For example, a rural school superintendent was recently tasked with consolidating two eighth-grade classes at different schools into one middle school program. At one school, a group of parents objected to the bus commute that their youngsters would have; another group wanted to ensure that there was adequate course work for high school preparation.

At the other school, some parents objected to the newcomers who came in as a result of the consolidation. Some parents liked the plan but objected to the timing and wanted to postpone it until later. The school faculty and staff also raised various issues and concerns.

The superintendent needed to hear all of these concerns and weigh what might be best for all in the long term as well as the short term. Politically, the superintendent was being pressed by the school board to enact a smooth transition as quickly as possible. The situation was multifaceted, with individual and group needs that varied and were conflicting.

Desired outcomes could be attempted unskillfully or inappropriately through power and authority. If we consider the classroom management situation above, the teacher has several options to handle disruptive student behavior, but it is considered inappropriate to employ punitive or hurtful means to discipline a child. While a beating might result in a quiet child, the process would also produce potentially harmful consequences. In this respect, the way we get to a good end is as important as the outcome itself.

Right action and good ends are ethical concepts that focus on means and ends. But these two concepts are not mutually exclusive of each other. The ideal is to achieve good outcomes through right action. In practice, however, right action does not always yield the good that was intended. Later in this book, we will discuss how to consider right means and good ends in determining what action to take. But first we turn to what we need to consider in making judgments and to what causes angst in decision making.

ANTECEDENT FACTORS

Ethical judgments are based on a variety of factors relating to how we deliberate and decide. Basically, these factors can be classified as either antecedent or consequential.

Antecedent factors, such as one's family, education, and life experiences, occur prior to a decision being made. These factors might affect how the individual thinks about her or his values, language, customs, culture, and education. It is likely that an individual raised in a multiethnic working-class neighborhood would have different experiences compared with someone from a homogeneous rural community, shaping his or her thinking and decision making.

At the same time, individuals sharing religious beliefs and practices might have a common ideological grounding regardless of their class, race and ethnicity, gender, or national origin. For instance, two Catholics with different life experiences (e.g., a fifth-generation Polish American raised in Michigan and a recently emigrated Mexican American living in San Antonio) might share fundamental values and beliefs of Catholicism that shape their ethical judgments.

Similarly, someone of minority background (e.g., an African American) might feel greater affinity toward another minority (e.g., a Vietnamese American) despite where they were raised or what their specific ethnic origins are because of their immigrant experiences assimilating into American society. These antecedent factors relate to an individual's personal values and beliefs that in turn affect moral and ethical decision making.

Shaped by individual values, beliefs, and responsibilities, we have been taught both formally and experientially in ways that contribute to the assumptions that we bring to any given situation.

Suppose that as a teacher, you had a disagreement with your union representative, leaving you with a bad impression of teachers' unions in general. As a consequence, you interpret the motives and actions of the union representative in your building in a skeptical manner. If, on the other hand, your prior experiences with the union had been positive, you might be more open to the union and its representatives.

Our prior experiences and beliefs can sometimes be so powerful that they do not allow us to see anything other than what we already "know." For example, if faculty come to believe that students always take advantage of any rights, that strong belief might deter cultivating students' sense of autonomy and independence in school. Assumptions that we hold individually and collectively play into how open we are to new concepts. Fesmire (2003) reminded us,

> The feeling that something is good does not necessarily make it so, and the judgment that it is the good of this situation is a working hypothesis qualified by experimental confirmation or disconfirmation. (p. 97)

As such, leaders might begin by considering prior experiences and held assumptions in order to see differently and be more open to others' viewpoints.

Antecedent factors also include the professional duties and responsibilities of being a school administrator. An administrator's professional duty is to ensure that the youngsters attending school are served well. Included is the responsibility to uphold the policies and procedures of the school, district, educational association, or organization.

For example, in devising a student attendance policy, the principal would need to consider existing policies for not only the school but the district, county, and state. There might be regulations within one's professional educational organization that are antecedent to deciding what action to take.

Rules and regulations are meant to offer guidance, perhaps even governance, in situations where judgment takes place. Their role is to shift the judgment from the actual situation to the interpretation of the rule in the situation. In a case of alleged harassment, rules could define and clarify the phenomenon of harassment. These could initiate the process for determining when a situation meets its definition, guiding the action needed. The actual decision is not whether the situation is harassment, but does the situation meet the policy definition of harassment. As such, the rule guides an ethically tricky situation.

There might also be unwritten cultural norms within daily operations of the organization that are antecedent factors to be considered when making ethical decisions. New leaders may be unaware of organizational rituals, routines, and unspoken norms that affect their organizations. Consulting with those more knowledgeable about institutional culture, traditions, and changes would be beneficial. For example, a new principal might seek the advice of a twenty-five-year veteran teacher or an experienced school secretary before making organizational changes.

As with individual and group differences, personal and professional antecedents may not be aligned, causing ethical tensions to surface when deliberating what action to take and how to decide. How does one handle a decision where the professional expectations directly contradict one's personal beliefs or vice versa?

For example, many educators currently feel conflicted over having to teach within narrowly defined achievement expectations measured by standardized tests. Professionally, they believe in covering a much wider curriculum and being allowed more discretion to address their students' academic, social, emotional, and other needs. The belief in a more holistic curriculum and adapted instruction might conflict with the directive to apply a reform model for meeting annual yearly progress goals.

Examining these antecedent factors (personal, professional, organizational) can suggest the kinds of values, beliefs, and assumptions held by individuals within the organization and the likely ethical tensions that might exist.

CONSEQUENTIAL FACTORS

The second category of factors to consider in decision making is what will happen once a judgment is rendered. What might result from this decision? Who will be affected, and how might they be impacted? How many individuals will benefit? Will anyone suffer from the action? Are there unintended and intended consequences from this action? What are some immediate short-term effects, as well as long-term ones, to consider? Reflecting upon these questions is critical to making the best decision possible.

As our experiences broaden, we are better able to specify consequential factors. A teacher's experiences might be restricted to a particular classroom or grade level. With the experiences as grade-level chairperson or dean of students, the teacher would gain a broader perspective to make decisions for the entire school. Given specific administrator training and mentoring, the individual might be better equipped to consider a fuller spectrum of consequences resulting from an administrative action.

Likewise, a salesperson's experience and knowledge of the company may be expanded by a promotion into management. Assuming leadership responsibilities, that person might look differently at the work of other salespeople in the organization as well as be in touch with different functions such as marketing, production, and quality assurance that factor into operations. We do not necessarily make better decisions because of management positions; rather we are presented with a broader spectrum of the numerous consequences possible in the institution.

It should be noted that we bring all of our life experiences into the equation, not only our professional ones. That is, a teacher may be a soccer coach as well as a choral director. He might be a parent with several children, or she could be the oldest of several siblings spread across the country. These varied experiences enable the individual to consider consequences more broadly than someone with limited experiences in collaborating with others and coordinating group efforts.

As mentioned earlier, utilitarianism is a school of ethics that emphasizes the consequences for the majority. Philosophers also use the term *consequentialism* to designate this ethical system. It holds that happiness is the ultimate good and that the best acts are those that produce the greatest good for the greatest number. As such, it offers a quantifiable formula for determining what action should be taken. But as Kant noted, all situations do not necessarily fit such reasoning. Principles like freedom, justice, and equality might preempt any consideration of majority. Regardless how many benefit, violating universal principles requires our attention.

At times, antecedent and consequential factors seem to fit with each other, where life experiences, values, and beliefs are aligned with the outcomes we seek. Personal beliefs and professional expectations seem aligned consistently with each other toward goals that we can agree on. Our ideals are aligned sufficiently with our aims so that we can do what we believe to be right and strive toward outcomes that are desirable.

However, as collaborators, it is more likely that there will be clashes over varied values, beliefs, life experiences, and other factors. There may be individual needs that clash with group needs. Personal ideology might contradict professional expectations and result in opposition and unintended consequences. Such situations create difficult decisions and ethical dilemmas, requiring us to look more closely, reflect thoughtfully, and demonstrate leadership more broadly.

ETHICAL DILEMMAS

What is a dilemma? Rushworth Kidder (1995) stated that a dilemma is when two or more options are equally viable choices. In essence, we are looking at a situation where there might be several possible actions, none completely satisfying. Perhaps the choice benefits the majority but with significantly negative consequences for some individuals. Or a good outcome occurs at the expense of right process by suppressing all opposition or the right protocol produces mediocre results.

In any case, dilemmas require that leaders engage in careful analysis and discernment to arrive at ethical judgments. What personal and professional antecedent factors need to be considered? What consequences might result from the actions taken? What means have been suggested to arrive at the outcomes? Have we weighed all the factors related to the decision? Have we sufficiently thought through the positives and negatives that might result from our actions? Later in the book we describe an inquiry method for addressing these questions.

For now, it is enough to know that a dilemma exists when there are two or more equally valued choices in a situation. One path is taken at the expense of the other. That is, consequences may differ substantially depending upon the action taken. When choosing between two wrongs, then you will be faced with mitigating any harm done by the choice.

This actually raises the question of whether an ethical leader should be considering any course of action that is "wrong." We think that the reality of leadership is such that leaders often have to stretch their ethics around the particular circumstances at hand. Badaracco (2006) stated that this is about developing moral–ethical codes that are sufficiently "complex, varied, and subtle as the situations in which they often find themselves . . . [to enable] leaders to fully understand the complexities of the situations they face, to see them in the same terms as others do, and to communicate more powerfully and effectively" (pp. 33–34).

Discerning ethical tensions in a dilemma can be helpful in decision making. Suppose you interpret a problem as being primarily a conflict among varied beliefs about education. Then the strategies associated with working the problem will have to do with finding people's commonalities or deconstructing their beliefs. If, on the other hand, you perceive that the problem relates to what is best for the majority, then you might need to determine what is "best," who is "the majority," and what activities are associated with that determination. In chapter 2, we describe various sources of ethical tension and how to identify them.

DEMOCRATIC ETHICS

Demonstrating moral leadership requires what we have labeled "democratic ethics." This term does not mean political systems or political parties (e.g., conservatives or liberals, Democrats or Republicans). Neither is it particularly about constitutional rights (e.g., freedom of speech, right to assembly and protest) or citizenship responsibilities (e.g., voting; paying taxes; abiding by national, state, and local laws).

Instead, we adhere to John Dewey's view that "democratic ethics" refers to how leaders maximize the potential and growth of each person in the situation while ensuring that the groups to which individuals belong support their growth (Kramer, 2006a). This means that there is a synergy between individual and group, personal and professional, and means and ends. These aspects cannot be categorically separated from each other, because they are integral and affect each other.

In effect, we believe that when presented with ethical dilemmas, leaders need to involve as many people as possible in a democratic process. They should be gathering input, involving those concerned, getting issues clarified, and negotiating a resolution that does not separate winners from losers. Leaders can promote democratic practices while negotiating the myriad of possible consequences that could result from taking action.

This can be a time for school organizations and their members to grow. Conversely, it can be a time when they are stymied and debilitated through formulaic or conditioned responses (LaMagdeleine & Kramer, 1998). We speak more about this in chapter 6, where we describe democratic leadership, and in chapter 7, where we present an inquiry method to be applied to complex ethical problems.

SUMMARY

In this chapter, we introduced the reader to key concepts related to ethics and ethical decision making. Tracing the Greek origins of our Western philosophy, *utilitarianism* proposes considering the "greatest happiness for all," whereas *deontology* advocates acting from one's duty. In ethical language, we distinguished *right* (means) from *good* (ends). Making an ethical judgment requires consideration of *antecedent* and *consequential* factors that relate to individuals and groups. Notably, ethical dilemmas occur when two or more options are equally viable but pose conflicts because of one's personal, professional, and organizational values. Defining key concepts in ethical language offers ways to think about democratic ethics for deliberation and decision making.

TWO

Ethical Tension, Judgment, and Consequences

In an essay titled "Law and Manners" (1924), English jurist John Fletcher Moulton placed ethics as the middle ground between the law, which required obedience, and total freedom of expression. He called ethics "obedience to the unenforceable," in which

> there is no law which inexorably determines our course of action, and yet we feel that we are not free to choose as we would. . . . It grades from a consciousness of a duty nearly as strong as positive law, to a feel that the matter is all but a question of personal choice. (Moulton as quoted in Kidder, 1995, p. 67)

Useful and pragmatic, this definition reminds us that ethics involves negotiating or deliberating a middle ground where there might not be a clear-cut choice. We may find ourselves deliberating between what we believe to be our duty and what we prefer to do. Or we must choose between values that are personally important and those sanctioned by our professional organization. Weighing these choices can create stress and tension as we decide what we ought to do.

In this chapter, we describe four commonly acknowledged sources of ethical tension and provide the philosophical thinking about each source. Conflicts can arise when people operate from these different sources as illustrated in educational settings. We advocate the need to understand these sources of ethical tension in order to negotiate workable resolutions and make reasoned judgments.

FOUR SOURCES OF ETHICAL TENSION

As an overview, Figure 2.1 depicts the four sources of ethical action that can create conflict. The first source, *duties-based ethics*, is based upon law and rules. It is ethical thinking that comes from an authority, such as religious precepts (e.g., the Ten Commandments, the Five Pillars of Islam) or government (e.g., the U.S. Constitution and the Bill of Rights). Such authority spells out the duties of a group member or citizen, that is to say, what a good person is responsible for doing in society. "At the heart of this morality is the idea of law which prescribes what is legitimate or obligatory" (Dewey, 1930, pp. 280–281).

But this ethical system relates to more than what has been legislated or is legal; it aims at that which is governed by principles to be upheld by all regardless of consequences. Often, we refer to duties-based ethics as

Figure 2.1.

deontological or *universalist* ethics, based on the Greek word *deon*, which means obligation.

The second source, *desires-based ethics*, refers to that which we desire or want. If we desire something, we probably believe that it would be "good" for us to have that something. For example, if we want quality educational opportunities for ourselves, we might likely advocate it for everyone. Dewey reminds us that what is good is relative, depending upon the historical context and subject to change based on the time, place, and circumstance of the situation.

Using this logic, a desires-based system would be any type of ethical system based on the final outcome, because it is attempting to define an ultimate good end. For this reason, it is also known as ends-based (*teleological*) ethics, based on the Greek word *telos*, meaning end or purpose.

A third source of ethical tension arises as we consider the individual characteristics or qualities of a person. Usually identified as *virtue ethics*, this source considers such questions as what makes a good person, what character traits or dispositions might they demonstrate, and how do those characteristics relate to the quality of judgments they might make. These questions arise from the behavior of virtuous persons.

Athenassoulis (2004) explained that "[i]nstead of asking what is the right act here and now, virtue ethics asks what kind of person should I be in order to get it right all the time." When we begin to discuss ethics from this viewpoint, we are considering a person's whole life and what makes for goodness. Virtue ethics, like trait theory, describes the qualities of a good person.

We describe the fourth source of ethical tension as *good society ethics*, which recognizes that we do not live alone or isolated from others. Rather, we are part of an ever-widening circle of social groupings—our immediate and extended families, occupational or professional associations, religious affiliations, geographic collectives, and so on. Looking at these social groupings, we can readily see ethical qualities within the group affiliations. Conflicts arise when we as individuals differ from our group, as well as when we are torn among different groups' expectations. Good society ethics asks that we consider what is good for the group, the expectations of group membership, and the rights and responsibilities within the group and among groups within society.

In the next section of this chapter, we present the language and logic of each source of ethical tension in greater detail. Some key philosophers are identified in discussing duties-based, desires-based, virtue, and good society ethics. We also show how conflicts occur among these four sources and where judgment comes into play in determining what action to take.

DUTIES-BASED ETHICS (THE DEONTOLOGICAL/UNIVERSALIST SYSTEM)

When you think about duty, do you think of your role as a citizen or as a community member? Or what about your obligations as an educator, school administrator, or professional? Perhaps you think first about your personal duties in your family as a spouse, parent, child, or sibling. Roles such as citizen, educator, professional, or family member have specific duties and responsibilities associated with them.

All duties can be defined by external and internal factors. Our affiliated groups (e.g., professional organizations, political affiliations, social clubs, church denominations) define the roles and responsibilities of their members. These external factors are different from how we ourselves might interpret those roles and responsibilities, which are internal factors.

Further, duties can be thought of as either obligation or privilege. To what extent does the word *duty* imply an obligation or a burden when considering the responsibility to fulfill it? Conversely, do you consider the duty an honor or a privilege? Both obligation and privilege might determine how we think of our duty and fulfill our responsibilities.

Ethicists draw from the Greek word *deon* (duty) to name deontological, or duties-based, ethics. Those who operate from this ethical system often have very strong beliefs coupled with a sense of responsibility and commitment to meet the expectations prescribed by their duties. Such strength of conviction can result in strong action, for example, demonstrating religious zeal or political activism on issues such as quality of life, the environment, war, poverty, and social engagement.

In the world of duties-based ethics, belief spawns a sense of duty, and duty spawns behavioral action. Prussian philosopher Immanuel Kant (1724–1804) helped us make the connection among these three aspects— belief, duty, and behavior.

Duties-based ethics is probably best encapsulated in Kant's work, *Fundamental Principles of the Metaphysics of Morals*, published in 1785. Kant proposed that a moral action was done out of a sense of duty rather than by following one's inclinations or desires. Such action was taken without regard for outcomes.

Ethical decision making was a rational application of reason, and reason should be able to lead to moral precepts (*maxims*, as he called them). Using reason, one could work out what ought to be done. We specifically use the terms *belief* and *behavior* here because Kant saw ethical duty as an expression of intent, coming from inside the person.

He distinguished ethical from juridical duty, in which we are externally constrained by legal consequences. Ethical duty is that which we do because it fulfills our beliefs about what we ought to do.

Consider two individuals who drive within the speed limit. One might do so believing that it is an ethical duty ("I ought to follow the speed limit to be a safe driver"), whereas the other individual drives at the speed limit because she does not wish to be ticketed. According to Kant's way of thinking, intention and belief determine which of the two drivers might be more likely to speed.

By separating ethical from legal arguments, Kant was able to describe what we ought to do all the time, not based on some external rule that was imposed, but on something inherent, namely, that which we believe to be good. The task then was to determine moral precepts that were universal and could be applied to all. These were what Kant called *imperatives*, meant for everyone to follow.

Further, he argued that our ethical aims were of a higher order than legal ones because legal aims were for controlling our behaviors within a given time and place. For example, some schools have dress codes that do not allow students to wear any jewelry, hats, bandannas, or other accessories; not all schools have such restrictions. These kinds of restrictions are contextually specific, therefore not universal. If a student goes to a different school, she or he must abide by the dress code of that school.

What, then, makes a moral precept a "universal" imperative? Kant distinguished two types of imperatives—*hypothetical* and *categorical*. Hypothetical imperatives are formulated as contingencies, for example, saying "If you don't want to get a speeding ticket, then you should not drive in excess of the speed limit." Another hypothetical imperative is "You should only wear clothing prescribed by the dress code if you don't want to get sent to the office."

By contrast, categorical imperatives imply actions taken always and everywhere and therefore are universally applicable. MacIntyre (1966) in paraphrasing Kant explains:

> "Act according to a maxim which can be adopted at the same time as a universal law." Categorical Imperative is a moral rule without exceptions, and we are not to be concerned with the possible unintended consequences of such an application. (p. 194)

We must follow this type of imperative, and it must apply to everyone, everywhere, and at all times. If you adopted the categorical imperative to treat others with dignity and respect, then it assumes persons have dignity and should be respected accordingly.

To test whether this is a categorical imperative, consider its negation. Could you treat someone poorly because they treated you poorly? Or could you treat people with dignity only if and when you felt like it? If that were the case, then no one could trust that dignity and respect would be present in human relations. This imperative would not meet Kant's test for being universally applied.

Another example of a categorical imperative is Kant's admonishment that humans should be treated as ends, not as means. That is, humans should always be treated with respect, and we should not use other people for our own gain. Such an imperative is typical of Kant, who believed in human dignity and expounded on this belief in his writing. It is the reason many current philosophers and ethicists feel a kinship with him today.

However there are numerous criticisms raised against Kant's thinking. The basic test of whether we operate morally is that we do our duty to the categorical imperatives we hold. According to MacIntyre (1966), Kant paid no attention to either context or consequences when assessing these imperatives. Without regarding possible consequences or analyzing actions taken congruent to those beliefs, a person might be inclined to rigidly conforming to the categorical imperative.

Suppose a friend provided you with classified information and asked that you protect his privacy by not disclosing the source. If an officer of the law were to demand that you reveal the source of your information, Kant's system of compulsory rules would not allow you to lie. In this case, you would not be able to keep your informant's confidentiality and tell the truth at the same time.

Another criticism is that while Kant speaks about acting "out of duty," we do not necessarily know what someone else's maxims are. In business dealings, we would not be able to distinguish a person who is genuinely honest from a reluctantly honest person "who deals fairly only out of desire for a good business reputation and would cheat if a sale opportunity arose" (O'Neill, 1991, p. 177). The behaviors of the two persons would be the same but their motivation and intentions might differ. As such, we can look only at the outward signs of conformity to maxims of duty rather than at what might have motivated that action.

The most common charge against Kant's ethics was made by Hegel, Marx, and others who alleged that a categorical imperative is "empty, trivial, or purely formal, and identifies no principles of duty" (O'Neill, 1991, p. 181). Hegel pointed out that Kant's moral law needed content and that such content was socially determined by the community in which a person lived. Moreover, the community might have a structure and impetus of its own that extends beyond individual choices. Issuing a similar critique, Marx suggested that more significant than individual choices and principles were the inevitable historical developments generated by economic forces.

Despite these criticisms, duties-based ethics remains an important consideration in leadership decisions because of the internal, deeply seated beliefs that people hold, as well as because of the responsibilities that people perceive to be part of whatever role they are playing. Conflicts often occur because people operate from what they believe to be their ethical duty in fulfilling their roles and responsibilities.

Suppose that as school principal, you seek to revise the math curriculum. Faculty members hold varied viewpoints about teaching mathematics in terms of what textbooks, assessments, and technology to use and how best to deliver such a curriculum. Some teachers strongly believe that a traditional math program is essential for the students; the belief forms a categorical imperative that all should follow. Other teachers believe that using an integrated math program will inspire more students, push the talented ones to do better, and keep the less talented ones engaged. Their categorical imperative is opposite that of the first group of teachers.

Which group is correct? Each group of teachers holds strong beliefs shaped by their educational background and experiences. Their entrenchment in these beliefs might make it almost impossible to adopt any curriculum that the entire school can agree upon and implement. Leading the faculty, you feel obligated to make changes and you declare, "The math teachers can't seem to come to any agreement, so I will decide about the math curriculum." Your action could alienate one group, disenfranchise the faculty, or undermine any meaningful school reform.

This example illustrates how differences in beliefs about duty and their associated categorical imperatives are a source of ethical tension. As a leader, you need to attend to the varied beliefs, values, and related senses of duty among your school members if conflicts are to be prevented and workable solutions made. Not paying attention to the categorical imperatives that others carry can result in the leader suffering the consequences of these deeply held beliefs.

DESIRES-BASED ETHICS (THE TELEOLOGICAL/UTILITARIAN SYSTEM)

Desires relate to what we seek or want as a result of our actions. Ethicists refer to the Greek *telos* (end) and call this ethical system *teleologica*, or ends based.

It is also known as utilitarianism, as devised by the English philosopher Jeremy Bentham (1748–1832). In establishing the "greatest happiness" principle, Bentham argued that actions should be judged on the results achieved, as summarized in the phrase "the best for the most." Quite simply, utilitarians seek to maximize desired ends for the majority of people. Given a situation with moral choices, they would argue that "the right thing to do is that which is likely to produce the greatest happiness for the greatest number of people" (Thompson, 2003, p. 67).

What makes teleological ethics so attractive to decision makers? First, there is a sense of caring that comes with this reasoning. After all, don't we appreciate another person's consideration of our own particular situation? Focusing on what is "best for the most" implies that we care about maximizing positive outcomes for most of the people. We look for a positive outcome for most of the group, demonstrating that we care for the well-being of the group as well as for the individuals in the group.

Second, this ethical system offers a practical principle for leaders to do what is best for the majority of their constituents. Its rationale goes along with the democratic notion that the majority rules. The logic is easy to understand and justify. Acting according to the desires of the majority can feel like the most efficacious way, and possibly the most politically safe way, to lead a diverse group of people.

Here is an example of how desires-based ethics might work. A business is trying to decide what kind of health care should be offered to employees. As CEO, you know that most of your employees are young, fit, and generally healthy. If you negotiate an employee health plan based on this, each of your employees will save a great deal of money because of the low cap on dollars required for the plan. Such savings could reduce liability for insurance or offer an enhanced retirement plan.

Taking such action would be considered very utilitarian. It is mutually advantageous for the company and the employees, representing what is best for the most. Even if one of the employees needs more than what is covered in the insurance, it still meets the utilitarian standard of "best for the most."

But here is the limitation with this ethical system. If one of your employees is diagnosed with a treatable but very long and expensive illness, the health insurance plan might not afford the coverage necessary, or that individual might incur a tremendous expense to be treated. Here, the needs of the one are not considered in the equation. Would it be right that the rest of the employees be able to save money at the expense of one employee's ability to get full coverage? Most of us recognize that our health situation could change at a moment's notice. The employee who is robustly healthy one day but in serious need the next will not be served if the utilitarian standard is applied.

How do utilitarian ethicists answer the questions raised by this example? Bentham argued that by maximizing that which brings the greatest good to the greatest number, we are actually serving society as a whole. The rationale is very useful for policy makers who seek to maximize collective impact, but what about those in the minority?

The health care example could be mitigated by asking, "Isn't it better for all of us to prepare for more care than we probably need at this time?" Such thinking is mutually advantageous to the employees who would be covered for the singly unpredictable health event, as well as to the company with its employees satisfied with the benefits received. It might even benefit the insurance provider with more money up front to invest and be ready for the company's more significant health care needs.

There are other critiques of desires-based ethics. If we follow this system of ethics to its logical end, then we might look out for only our own best interests. That is, we would want to make sure that our interests were aligned with those of the majority. But suppose our views were different from the majority. Could we support a minority point of view? To what extent could we consider the needs and desires of those with little power and influence? These are questions that raise issues with majority-rules logic.

A second critique is that desires-based ethics is extremely dependent upon an analysis of consequences for its value judgments. If we were interested only in consequences, then what about the universal principles that are valued? Do we want to operate in a world that is so consequentialist that good cannot be determined until after the fact? While consequences should be considered in ethical decision making, what about duty and universal principles? Overreliance on consequences in desires-based ethics also raises questions about "what is good?" and "who determines it?"

Finally, this kind of utilitarian thinking is susceptible to a contingency analysis, which poses "what if " questions. These are important to consider, but keep in mind that what looks like the best option for the majority right now might not be or might change over time.

CONTRASTING DUTIES WITH DESIRES

Before taking action in a situation, a leader needs to contemplate what people believe (duties) as well as what they want to achieve (desires). This is not to say that individuals will not rise above their personal desires to fulfill their responsibilities, but there are times when one's perceived duties may conflict with another's most ardent desires in such a way that it is impossible to see any convergence of possible action.

Take, for example, the federal No Child Left Behind Act of 2001 requiring that all children meet minimum standards of learning. Most educators may agree that this is a desirable end. Most may even commit to that duty as part of being a professional educator. But suppose you are working with children whose lives are so fragile that just getting them to school seems to be an accomplishment. More than 20 percent of American children live in poverty, and many educators, while agreeing with the ultimate goal of No Child Left Behind, feel that the physical and emotional needs of the children at risk are paramount.

The desire to comfort and provide safety may come first, thus conflicting directly with the stated priority to meet academic standards. Add the obligation that the school must demonstrate having made student achievement gains each year to avoid being restructured for missing annual yearly progress (AYP) goals. The legal and ethical consequences may force school leaders to weigh what would be the best approach to ensure quality education for all children within the school or system.

VIRTUE ETHICS

In chapter 1, we discussed right actions (means) and good results (ends). We asked, what is the right thing to do? As well, we needed to consider the good that was the aim. Both duties-based and desires-based ethics require that actions taken be judged as right or wrong. But there are other equally important ethical questions. For example, is it possible to know the actual goodness of a person? Should we have some way of judging people's character, not just because they meet their responsibilities or maximize the good for the majority? In essence, we are asking, what does it mean to be a good person?

To answer such questions, ethicists have relied upon Greek philosophers Plato (ca. 428–354 BCE) and Aristotle (ca. 384–322 BCE), who attempted to define ethics associated with questions about what makes a person moral or good. This system of ethics became known as virtue ethics. A virtuous citizen of Plato's time was one who fulfilled his (emphasis on the masculine) role in the society, be he slave or master. Regardless of his role, the citizen was expected to be the best that he could be. Such role fulfillment was deemed to be a demonstration of good character.

In contemporary times as well, we generally view individuals who fulfill their roles and responsibilities as being virtuous. But might a thief or a criminal be considered "virtuous" under this designation if he or she is the "best" in his or her role? Considering particular ways of living and acting, ethicists needed to look beyond individual characteristics or qualities.

Plato's student, Aristotle, went so far as to discuss habits of ethical behavior that would be susceptible to analytical reason. Plato felt that, for a man to learn to discern the ethical, he would need to study the sciences and mathematics. Aristotle strongly disagreed and believed that experience, combined with the right beliefs, would result in ethical wisdom.

Virtue was an elaborate set of calculations based upon an ideal person, for which Aristotle gave a mathematical quality. He defined it as the midpoint between two nonvirtues—one of excess and the other of deficiency—known as the doctrine of the means (Rowe, 1991). Accordingly, Aristotle saw the virtue of prudence existing between the deficiency of miserliness and the excess of the spendthrift. Similarly, courage exists at the midpoint between recklessness and cowardice.

Perhaps the most significant modern virtue ethicist is Alasdair MacIntyre who, influenced by the writings of Aristotle, advocated a return to virtues as a way of connecting with what was historically considered "good." In addition, virtues help sustain practices that are consistent with those good ends. MacIntyre (1984) believed that virtues help keep the good traditions of a society intact while weeding out practices that are antithetical to social norms. He wrote:

Lack of justice, lack of truthfulness, lack of courage, lack of the relevant intellectual virtues—these corrupt traditions, just as they do those institutions and practices which derive their life from the traditions of which they are the contemporary embodiments. (p. 223)

For MacIntyre, the modern tendency to avoid calling some characteristics "good" has resulted in a lack of clarity in ethical language and a disturbing lack of social unity in terms of identifying those moral equivalents to which we should aspire.

In leadership, we often see virtue ethics in the guise of trait theory, which attempts to describe the good leader with particular traits. We might see that an individual having character traits such as boldness, determination, commitment, courage, and compassion might be assessed as a capable and effective leader.

This is often evident in the process of selecting a new principal or superintendent. While the job listing for an administrative position specifies necessary requirements and lists the responsibilities of the job, the selection committee might discuss the various candidates based upon their perceived virtues. Reviewing applicants for the position, a committee member might comment, "Even though [the candidate] doesn't have a lot of experience, I felt his honesty would make him a successful leader." Someone else might identify another desirable trait: "Her references attest to her caring for the faculty and staff. That is the kind of leader we need here." The selection committee might choose based upon speculation about the applicant's character traits (e.g., honesty, caring) rather than upon capabilities and competence.

Virtue ethics is probably most visible when a person's character is called into question. Suppose that a leader is seen as trustworthy and loyal, as demonstrated by her dedication to the group that she serves. By contrast, another leader who is not trusted may have earned this attribution because of an inconsistent application of policies and procedures, a haphazard interpretation of the rules, or a lack of follow-through. The assessment can be particularly problematic when we associate certain traits with general characteristics, such as one's social class, race and ethnicity, gender, age, family background, religion, or the like.

Virtue ethics allows us to move away from the duties-versus-desires reasoning traditionally found in ethical decision making. In this system of ethics, our actions are based upon what good people should do. Take the idea that good people should make good friends. They do things for each other based upon friendship, not upon whether they get something out of the relationship. They act out of caring toward their friends rather than because of benefits accrued. Such a belief is grounded in the qualities that exist long before any action is taken. This is one of the strengths of virtue ethics.

GOOD SOCIETY ETHICS

Sociologist Robert Bellah and his colleagues explored a form of virtue ethics that would lead to good individual lives. In *Habits of the Heart* (1991), they described a "language of individualistic achievement and self-fulfillment that often seems to make it difficult for people to sustain their commitments to others" (Bellah, Madsen, Sullivan, Swidler, & Tipton, 1991, p. vi). Realizing that a focus on only the individual could lead to cultural narcissism and the inability to manifest compassion, they later proposed an ethical language that accounted for group action and institutional responsibility, which they called "good society."

Usually ethicists discuss this source of ethics by describing groups and their relationship with individual members. Specifically, what should an individual expect from the groups to which he or she belongs? What should the group expect from the individual? To answer these questions, a good group is often described using virtue terms (e.g., just, fair, caring, productive) as its features. For our purposes, we begin with the definition that a group is a social construct—individuals linked by common interest or affiliation. The "good" group then should maximize the abilities of its members to meet those common interests. How is this done? Let's look at the concern for personal and mutual safety.

Suppose you live in a residential community and would like to ensure the safety of yourself and your family. To meet these requirements, you agree to a social contract with the larger community that involves giving up something to remain safe. You might give up free time in order to patrol the neighborhood and ensure that a steady watch is maintained.

Alternatively, you might agree to pay into a common fund for hiring someone to watch over the community. This is what cities and counties do by employing police or security officers to patrol and protect our neighborhoods. Whatever the choice, you have given up something in order that the group as a whole may benefit. This contractual arrangement with the group will regulate action, avoid conflict, and provide for the safety of all who live in the community.

Consider another example of a social contract. As an educator, you are a member of a teachers' union and must pay dues. While you may not like paying union dues, the membership enables you to have collective bargaining over individual negotiations in terms of pay, benefits, and working conditions. Union membership also offers you protection from being treated in an unseemly or unfair manner by a superior. You would expect that the union would intervene on your behalf in such cases, ensuring that due process is followed, providing for mediation, and advocating for your rights.

In this instance, the good group fulfills its contract with its members (e.g., providing collective bargaining and protecting rights), and a good individual member fulfills a responsibility to the group (e.g., paying union dues). Notice the reciprocity between a good individual and a good group.

However it is possible to use the same reasoning to justify a so-called prison state. The society offers safety and protection but only if the individual members agree to give up so many rights that their existence in it becomes oppressive. It is precisely this type of ethical problem that contemporary philosopher John Rawls (1971) sought to resolve. He proposed a means to determine a good society that would account for individuals being self-interested but still willing to participate in a social contract that might benefit others.

What would cause a person to act for the good of the whole rather than based exclusively on self-interest? Rawls proposed this hypothetical situation. Individuals could design an ideal society, revising the laws accordingly, but would operate under "a veil of ignorance." That is, they were required to construct the society without knowing their placement in the social hierarchy. They would not know their age, race, skin color, wealth, or social position. They would have no reference to any special interest group. Rawls posited that rational people would wish the best for the least members because, under the "veil of ignorance," they might be placed at the bottom of the social order.

Accordingly, such a society would be "good" because it met two criteria. First, every individual would have the right to the greatest liberty possible. Second, social and economic inequalities would be justifiable only if they benefited those who were socially or economically disadvantaged. These criteria have been used to justify freedom of the press and progressive tax systems. In establishing social contracts on this basis, Rawls argued that there would be a balance between the rights of the individual and the needs of the society.

Critics of Rawls cite the hypothetical nature of the situation, arguing it to be unrealistic and useless. Even Rawls admitted that other principles besides self-interest might govern how individuals decide to distribute resources, share benefits, or suffer consequences (Kymlicka, 1991). However, Rawls did define a good individual and can link the contractual arrangement between the good individual and the good society. Moreover, his premise that each person matters and is entitled to equal consideration is endorsed in American democracy.

CONTRASTING VIRTUE AND GOOD SOCIETY ETHICS

Attempting to apply virtue ethics to the good society, there is an assumption that good people will necessarily build a good society. While it might be argued that good people will influence the society in which they are members, describing the elements of the good society breaks down when limited to descriptions of individuals.

Consider the virtue of honesty. Would it be reasonable to expect that honest people working together would make honesty the norm in the workplace? It may be likely, but there could be circumstances that might restrict the honesty among certain individuals in the group. Total honesty and trust among workers might be hampered because of past relationships; work experiences; new leadership; or changes in power, authority, and organization. The virtue of honesty might not translate directly into honesty in the work group.

It should be no surprise that individual and group interests often conflict. John Dewey proposed that each of us has our own perception of what we personally desire, and most of us can justify taking care of ourselves before considering the group's needs.

For example, in Minnesota, mass transit is only minimally available. The metropolitan areas are nearing transportation gridlock due to inadequate highways and more cars on the roads. Yet many legislators are not willing to support mass transit, citing that their constituents do not wish to give up driving their cars or pay the extra taxes for light rail or other transit. The debate is usually cast as the government encumbering the freedoms of individuals through higher taxes and asking people to ride buses and trains. It is precisely this type of public–private conflict that legislators must face if the situation is to be reformed.

In educational leadership, an attempt to reconcile the tensions between good groups and good individuals can be seen most clearly in the writings of Robert J. Starratt, professor emeritus at Boston College. Dr. Starratt has been exploring the application of virtues to both schools and school leaders for at least the past twenty-five years.

In *Building the Ethical School* (1994), Starratt offered the three virtues of care, justice, and critique for structuring a good school environment. A good school must ensure that there is a caring environment, provide justice and fairness, and promote openness to critical inquiry and analysis. Reminding us of the continual struggle involved in building these kinds of schools, Starratt stated that

> virtue is not something we achieve and then continue to possess. We continue to be capable of doing evil. Virtue is always out in front of us to be achieved; it involves a perpetual doing. (pp. 135–136)

Writing about *Ethical Leadership* (2004), Starratt described the virtuous leader by presenting a "morality play" about a principal who is worried about how faculty provide instruction, especially for youngsters with special needs. In several reflective talks with a mentor, the principal is able to define his authentic beliefs and identify his responsibilities as a human being, administrator, and citizen. Three virtues—responsibility, authenticity, and presence—form the building blocks for this leader's deliberation in working the ethical tensions. By focusing on these dynamics, Starratt showed us not only how complicated school leadership can be but that virtuous leadership is always under pressure.

While not specifically looking for congruence or dissonance between the school group attributes (care, justice, and critique) and the leadership virtues (responsibility, authenticity, and presence), one can ask the question, how might individual responsibility and authenticity be mitigated by the need for just rules in a caring environment? Starratt neither denies nor endorses such tensions, but he is very interested in how the school leader might affect the goodness of a school.

CONFLICTING SOURCES OF ETHICAL TENSION

Ethical tension can be present in any given situation and can exist between and within any of the four sources. We have contrasted duties with desires and have illustrated virtues of individuals clashing with groups. There is also the tension that occurs when virtues of either individuals or groups clash with our duties and desires. This is characterized as the clash between who we are (virtue and good society ethics) and what we believe or seek to accomplish (duties-based or desires-based ethics).

In Figure 2.2, we illustrate the contrasting tensions that occur across the different sources. For example, there is the tension between virtues and desires that may occur when one's personal sense of excellence and integrity (specific virtues) clashes with achieving a particular goal within a limited time period (ends or outcomes). It may also occur when personal values conflict with desires of the majority to which one belongs. While we might acknowledge our affiliation with the group, our personal values are at odds with what is desired by the group.

The second contrasting tension is between conflicting desires and outcomes among varied groups that we term "good society." As noted earlier, each of us is a member of multiple social groupings, affiliations, and associations that can be personal, professional, or cultural. The desires and expectations of these varied groups may not be aligned, pulling us in different directions and creating stress as we decide what we desire. This tension can be thought of as a clash of good society ethics with desires-based ethics.

The third tension is similar. The clash between different group affiliations may play out in what is deemed best for the whole group (good society ethics) in contrast with the roles, responsibilities, and obligations of the members (duties-based ethics). Consider what happens when one's obligation to the family clashes with one's professional duties and responsibilities. Choosing between two equally important commitments can be stressful and challenging.

Lastly, we see the tension between virtue ethics and duties, as for example, when one faces a choice between telling the truth (the virtue of honesty) or remaining loyal to the group (fulfilling one's duty). It is also present when we personally disagree with a fundamental rule or law. Our obligation as a citizen is to follow the laws of the land, but if we are ethically opposed to a specific law, then tension between virtue and duty might exist. As illustrated, the sources of ethical tension deal with our perceived duties and desires as well as our definitions of the good person and the good society.

JUDGMENTS AND CONSEQUENCES

In the process of working through these ethical tensions, judgment is probably the most important skill that leaders can bring to a situation. We are expected to begin by gathering available information, reflecting upon the needs of the individuals involved, and considering probable outcomes. Having weighed the evidence and consequences, we are obliged to make the best possible decision given the circumstances.

What informs that judgment? Typically our judgments are framed by one or more of the ethical tensions described above. If we have staunch beliefs about how we want something to turn out or we feel obligated toward specific actions because of professional responsibility, then we might operate from particular virtues that apply to the situation at hand.

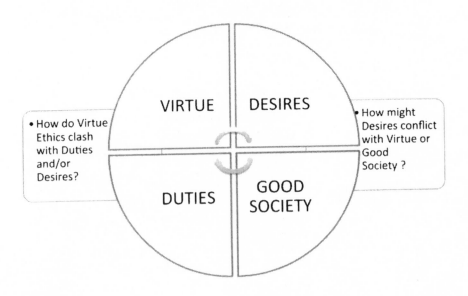

Figure 2.2.

Hopefully we can remain open to others' views and not be obstinate to all compromise or excessively proud and stubborn in our own convictions. Perhaps we recognize the importance of collaboration with the community groups that we serve. But we also acknowledge that not all desires can be met and that subgroups might hold conflicting views. We might seek to understand the larger group's views and values in the particular situation. Such beliefs inform the judgments that we make.

We must also consider the consequences of our actions, specifically what we think is going to happen. The consequences may be internal or external, positive or negative. For example, suppose you choose to lie to a dear friend. As a result of this action, you feel guilty, a consequence that is internalized.

An external consequence is the social approbation for an action. If you are publicly censured for your lying, this would be a negative external consequence, which might deter you from behaving in this manner again. Conversely, social approval or praise might encourage your actions, but should you always act in ways that garner praise and popularity? Ethical judgment requires weighing the possible positive and negative consequences of a given action.

When faced with a challenging situation causing an ethical dilemma, it is expected that the leader will work through a process of reasoning and reflection to make a final judgment about what to do. In Figure 2.3, we sketch how ethical decision making might occur from an initial problem through working toward some action. This process model shows how the four sources of ethical tension can be integrated in our deliberations when considering what action is to be taken.

As we embark on the process of ethical deliberation and decision making, it is helpful to remember the playwright Sophocles's advice in the Greek tragedy *Antigone*. The heroine Antigone has been condemned to death for her actions, and while she did not waver in her convictions, she demonstrated struggling with the complexity of her situation. According to Badaracco (2006), Sophocles advised us that

> good deliberation is a messy process. It goes back and forth, often zigzagging among feelings, thoughts, facts, and analysis. It is discursive rather than linear. It doesn't forget the past. It also looks forward, with vivid imagination, to possible consequences. Good deliberation acknowledges clear duties as well as open-ended responsibilities. It weighs and judges moral principles before applying them and again after applying them. And serious reflection does not seize a single grand principle—like duty to country or duty to the gods and family— and let it obliterate other considerations. (p. 175)

Problem/situation
What has initiated the need for description?

Information gathering
What is necessary information and data?

Ethical systems
What are the sources of ethical tension? Duties-based versus Desires-based.
Virtue Ethics versus Good society, or some other combination?

Judgment/Discernment
Can a judgment be made? Is there adequate information? If we do not have sufficient
information, how might we reconsider and reflect upon the problem further by using the
four ethical systems?

Consequences
What are the likely consequences? What are actual anticipated and unanticipated
outcomes?

Resolution/Reflection
Is the problem resolved as a result of action taken?
If not, how might we reconsider and revise our decision?

Figure 2.3.

SUMMARY

In this chapter, we identified four distinctive sources of ethical tension as people deal with each other. First, duty-based ethics (also known as deontological ethics) relates to one's personal and professional duties that prescribe universal principles to be upheld by all (universalist). Second, desires-based ethics (teleological, or ends-based, ethics) focuses on the best for the majority (utilitarian). The third source of ethical tension emphasizes the individual's character and behavior (virtue ethics), contrasting with the fourth source, a group perspective on character and behavior (good society ethics).

Each source of ethical tension forms a system of assumptions and beliefs used in decision making that can clash when people operate from different ethical perspectives. Conflicts can occur in any situation, can be internal as well as external, and can exist among all four of the sources.

To work through these conflicts, leaders need to employ sound judgment and consider the consequences of each action. We briefly sketched a process model showing how the sources of ethical tension are embedded within deliberation. Discursive rather than linear, deliberation goes back and forth. It is no wonder that conflict resolution often looks difficult, messy, and irreconcilable.

THREE
Religion and Religious Attitudes

Many of us find it challenging to discuss how religion, particularly our own religious beliefs, relates to our professional lives. Some individuals view religious ideology to be deeply personal, not appropriate in professional settings. Others hold the view that public servants like school leaders should discriminate between religious and secular matters, separating church and state. Still others do not see any division between acting ethically and professing a religious ideology in a public setting. Doing what is right and good means demonstrating their religious beliefs in daily life. In teaching about ethics and school leadership, we attempt to address these perspectives and believe them needed in a book about leadership and ethics.

Many ethical concerns relate back to our religious orientation and ideology. In chapter 2, we discussed sources of ethical tension, namely how one's duties might clash with one's desires, or how one's virtues might conflict with a view of a good society. These sources of tension can be greatly influenced by our religious beliefs and values about what makes a good person, what is right to do, and what defines a moral–ethical society.

As well, how we choose to decide about what action to take may be influenced by our particular religion. We might follow a creed like the Golden Rule from the Bible: "Always treat others as you would like them to treat you" (Matthew 7:12). Perhaps we might seek divine inspiration through contemplative meditation practices, as found in Hinduism or Buddhism. For these reasons, we believe it is necessary to clarify the role of our religious values and beliefs in conducting ethical deliberation and decision making as educators working in public school settings.

We start with a definition of religion and describe briefly how it has evolved as our society has become increasingly diversified and complex.

Consideration is given to how our religious traditions inform the moral–ethical choices we make and determine what codes of conduct might contribute to our actions. By contrasting different religions, we highlight the variability among ideologies across and within religions.

Consideration is given to the religious freedom made available by our U.S. Constitution and practiced in American society. To move beyond the legal domain, we refer to John Dewey's distinction between religion and religious attitude, which enables us to be more open to inquiry. Finally, we address the work expected of school administrators who need to honor religious freedom while accommodating diversity.

DEFINITION OF RELIGION

Derived from the Latin *ligo*, meaning "to tie or bind," the word *religion* originally meant being bound by vows to a particular way of life, as were *les religieux*, the monastics who took certain vows (Dewey, 1934, p. 23). Using the *Oxford Dictionary*, Dewey (1934) quoted the definition of religion to be "recognition on the part of man [sic] of some unseen higher power as having control of his destiny and as being entitled to obedience, reverence and worship" (p. 3).

In a more general sense, Fasching, deChant, and Lantigua (2011) suggested that religion can connote being obliged to whatever powers we believe might govern our way of life. Ancient peoples, for example, viewed nature with awe and revered the collective powers that provided life as well as destroyed it. Through myths and ritual, they honored the appropriate gods that brought a good harvest, fertility, prosperity, and victory in war. It was believed that failure to do so would bring famine, poverty, death, and destruction. The earliest religious stories were versions of how nature, either personified as gods, spirits, or magical forces, governed human destiny.

As tribal communities became less dependent upon nature and more complex in social organization, the view shifted from humans being arbitrarily at the whim of nature toward their being part of a divinely inspired cosmic plan. Customs or mores were regarded as sacred and unchangeable. The word *morality* was derived from the Latin root (*mos, mores*) that meant "customs" of the people. Fasching et al. (2011) defined it this way:

> Morality is an inherent dimension of the sacred order of society. In large part, what gives a society social stability is the sense that its way of life is sacred and unchangeable. (p. 12)

Sociologist Emile Durkheim viewed religion as the "human response to the overwhelming (and therefore sacred) power of society upon which we depend for our existence," with religious myths supporting that sacredness and social stability (Fasching et al., 2011, p. 13). Tribal peoples honored their ancestors, revered totems, and recounted myths to bring about that social stability. In more complex societies, we find religion providing meaning for life and providing the stability needed to weather the inevitable uncertainties of contemporary living.

In a similar vein, Max Weber concurred that religion functioned to sanction the "routine order" of society, but he also proposed that it could at times bring about dramatic social change. For example, the Roman Catholic Church served to uphold the social order during the Middle Ages but was called into question by Martin Luther, who led the Protestant Reformation and challenged the church's proprietary establishment. A new religious order and authority were replacing what had been held to be sacred.

While religious practices have served to order and give meaning to our lives, secular ideologies, such as scientific reasoning and technology, have challenged them. For instance, geological discoveries have displaced creation myths, and the biological sciences, particularly research in genetics, have revolutionized current thinking about mind–body connections.

Fasching et al. (2011) described how science emerged, beginning as early as the seventeenth century, to replace religious stories of origin with secular ones and became the dominant view:

> In the nineteenth and twentieth centuries this way of viewing the world was spread to virtually all cultures around the globe through colonialism—the European political and economic domination of the world's cultures. At the beginning of the nineteenth century, it seemed as if the great missionary movements of Christianity, which accompanied colonialism around the globe, would overcome all other religions. By the end of the century, it was beginning to look as if science was replacing all religions and that religion itself would soon disappear. In this world, human beings were no longer supposed to be guided in their public life by their ancient sacred stories but by scientific and technical reason. (p. 48)

But that was not to be the case. The utopian belief that science and technology would lead to progress was severely compromised in World War II, culminating in the mass destruction of lives at Auschwitz and Hiroshima. "Technical experts were not supposed to raise ethical questions about mass death: they were supposed to follow orders with unquestioning obedience" (Fasching et al., 2011, pp. 55–56).

If through such bureaucratic rationalization we could condone acts of mass murder, then we needed moral–ethical principles to direct our lives. For that, as a people, we again turned back to religious traditions, institutions, and ideology, but with much greater variability and diversity, as evident in our global society.

RELIGIOUS TRADITIONS

As in the past, religious traditions promote values that specify the meaning of life. In Christianity, for example, redemption is found in the Kingdom of God through his son, Jesus Christ. A meaningful life can be achieved by following Jesus's teachings and living a similar life. For Buddhists, the inevitable suffering (*dukkha*) of human life can be ended and enlightenment (*nirvana*) attained, as demonstrated by the Buddha himself. In the Hindu ethical tradition that originated around 1500 BCE, meaning is to be found in who you are as well as in what stage of life you have reached in a defined caste. By following the natural order, a Hindu practitioner can generate positive effects (*karma*) and reap benefits in the next life (Bilimoria, 1991, p. 47).

Religious traditions, institutions, and ideology prescribe how we should live. For example, Judaism teaches that the right way is to observe the Torah, which are revelations of the will of God. In some 613 commandments, the Torah specifies roles and relationships (e.g., parent to child, husband to wife), laws, diet, and other rules for living. Among the best known are the Ten Commandments and the Levitical Code. A basic contribution of Judaism to the Western religious tradition is "that one worships God through decent, humane, and moral relations with one's fellows" (Kellner, 1991, p. 84).

Derived from the same roots as Judaism and Christianity, Islam is a theistic religion based on the belief that there is one God (*Allah*), and it includes prophets like Abraham, Moses, and Jesus. The Prophet Muhammad, the founder of Islam, taught that obedience to God required submission, which brought about unity, brotherhood, righteousness, and peace. A devout follower (*Muslim*) was expected to observe the Five Pillars of Islam, each a part of the right action that leads to becoming a good person.

By contrast, Buddhism is a nontheistic religion with a set of guidelines for individual spiritual development. Buddhist teachings are based on the Four Noble Truths, which define human suffering, its cause, its cessation, and the means to its end (Armstrong, 2001). The guidelines to end suffering are specified in the Eightfold Path, a code of conduct about right beliefs, ideals, words, deeds, livelihoods, efforts, thinking, and meditation. Through diligent commitment, a Buddhist practitioner can overcome the suffering caused by greed, hatred, and illusion while developing a way of life leading toward peace, joy, and enlightenment.

Variation of a given religion might occur among its branches or sects, where some followers take a more conservative interpretation of the religion than others do. Within the Jewish religion today, the Orthodox, Conservative, and Reform sects all accept the moral and ethical teachings of Judaism but differ in their observance of the ceremonial and ritual laws. Orthodox believers keep strictly to the traditional ceremonial regulations as found in the Torah, the teachings (*Talmud*), and other books by religious leaders. Conservative Jews, while recognizing Jewish ritual law, have chosen to adopt some modifications in practice. Reform Jews generally place less emphasis on the rituals and tend to use the teachings as general guiding principles, more in the spirit of the faith rather than the letter of the law.

Derivations of Christian morality vary not only from one denomination to another but among different sources of authority (Thompson, 2003). At the time of the Protestant Reformation, for instance, Luther challenged the authority of the Roman Catholic Church on the basis of the authority of the scriptures. Since that time, reason and conscience have played an important role in reexamining and exploring a Protestant's moral action.

Islamic sects can also vary by sources of authority. In the Middle East, the two largest sects of Muslims, the Sunnis and Shiites, formed after the Prophet Muhammad died and followers split among the successors. Notably, the Shiites uphold a Muslim tradition tied to the spiritual authority vested in the designated spiritual teacher (*imam*) or his representatives, acknowledged to be the custodian of its holy book (*Koran*) and the Prophet Muhammad's teachings (Nanji, 1991). Though less numerous than the Sunni, the Shiites have challenged them for religious and political leadership in parts of Saudi Arabia, Iran, Iraq, North Africa, and Pakistan.

The religious values of one specific tradition may apply to society in general, not only to the members of that religious persuasion. Christianity has had a prominent role in our country's history and culture, with societal practices viewed to be habitual and "natural." Evidence can be found in our coinage (e.g., "In God we trust"), our ceremonies (e.g., saying the pledge of allegiance), and our rituals (e.g., taking an oath of office using a Bible). But not all American citizens are of the Christian faith, and in a democratic society where freedom of religion is honored, they should not have to be.

A religious tradition might be so much a part of a social fabric that it is difficult to determine religious values and beliefs as contrasted with the moral–ethical values of that society. Hinduism, from as early as 1500 BCE, exemplifies not one specific religion but various religious traditions of the South Asian subcontinent, each defining the morally good life and specifying its right conduct. Indian ethics might be described as "the 'soul' of the complex spiritual and moral aspirations of the people, comingled with social and political structures forged over a vast period of time" (Bilimoria, 1991, p. 43). It represents a diversified collection of systems that have changed over time.

Branches or sects within a religious tradition can evolve across different societies as well as change over time. Although Buddhism originated in India, it took root in many Asian countries, creating varied sects like Chan Buddhism, which first arose in China and later became Zen practice in Japan. The cultures of India, China, and Japan contributed much to the development and evolution of Buddhism in those respective countries. Thus, as Thompson (2003) stated,

> it is not simply a matter of understanding the religious and cultural norms of each group, but of sorting out to which group a person is giving his or her loyalty at any one time. Such diversity also affects religions that cross cultures. (p. 164)

Adding to this complexity, each religious tradition may present seemingly contradictory moral and ethical directions. On the one hand, individuals are directed to follow religious precepts and be good in order to be justly rewarded. Thus, they should follow prudent reasoning and act in their own self-interest to be duly rewarded rather than punished. On the other hand, individuals are to uphold the ethical ideal of selflessness in caring for the well-being of others. Philosophers call this an appeal to "moral reason," to do what benefits others before oneself.

Which directive is correct? In *Religion and Moral Reason* (1988), philosopher Ronald Green proposed that there are stages of spiritual growth and development. The seemingly contradictory advice needs to be understood as different directions for individuals at varied stages:

> [S]tories of punishment and reward are meant for beginners in the moral and spiritual life, while the stories of selfless love and compassion are meant for those more advanced. (Fasching et al., 2011, p. 29)

Ultimately, it is hoped that one's religious tradition provides a comprehensive set of stories, rituals, and spiritual practices to support one's spiritual evolution.

In sum, we have attempted to present examples of how different religious traditions provide meaning and spiritual direction for our lives. This may be directed toward a teleological end that defines meaning and purpose in life. Or it may be in the form of codes of conduct or precepts to follow as deontological constraints on our actions. Depending on the religious tradition, these codes may vary according to different interpretations of the law, different branches or sects, or different governing authorities.

Religious institutions and ideologies have evolved over time and across distance, from the country of origin to the country of adoption. As we evolve in our thinking and reflection, so too does our understanding of religious ideology and the traditions directing our moral conduct and ethical action.

RELIGIOUS FREEDOM

The first article of the U.S. Bill of Rights states that "Congress shall make no law respecting an establishment of religion, or prohibiting the free exercise thereof," which enables individuals to worship as they see fit. Furthermore, they are entitled to not worship at all if that is their belief. By directive of our U.S. Constitution, the national government must permit full religious freedom to its citizens. In the years since America was founded, state governments have made similar provisions to protect religious freedom.

However in practice our religious tolerance as a society has been limited. Until the late 1960s, tolerance in the public school setting applied only to different kinds of Protestant religious expressions. Catholic practitioners historically found that public schools were sufficiently unfriendly to their tradition and chose to start a separate school system altogether (Strike, Haller, & Soltis, 1998). Non-Christian religious followers have been particularly marginalized for being nontheistic (e.g., Buddhist or Confucian beliefs), for observing prayers (e.g., praying five times a day as Muslims do), and for commemorating holy days other than Christian ones (e.g., the Jewish Sabbath beginning at sundown on Fridays).

Legally the U.S. Supreme Court has since ruled that conducting prayer or Bible readings in public school forums is in violation of the First Article of the Bill of Rights. Also illegal are acts such as endorsing a particular religion over another, promoting religion against being nonreligious, and proselytizing in public school settings.

What schools can legally do is provide transportation, books, and other materials, as well as support services, to religious schools. They may provide accommodations for students who have religious conflicts with aspects of the curriculum or for scheduling around religious observances. If schools permit nonreligious groups to use their facilities, then they must do the same for religious groups (Shapiro & Stefkovich, 2005).

DISTINGUISHING A RELIGIOUS ATTITUDE

Beyond the legal domain, how do we make moral–ethical decisions based upon our religious traditions? Dewey (1934) offered a helpful distinction between religion and the "religious." The noun *religion* "always signifies a special body of beliefs and practices having some kind of institutional organization, loose or tight" (p. 9). To differentiate, the adjective *religious* denotes "attitudes that may be taken toward every object and every proposed end or ideal" (p. 10). A "religious" attitude is much more general and can apply to that which is outside of organized or formal religion.

Illustrating the religious aspect of experience, Dewey related the story of a writer who, on the verge of a nervous breakdown, resolves to set aside time daily to relate his life to God. This reorientation brings him a sense of security and peace. While a particular religion is emphasized in this story in terms of the writer relating to a personal God, Dewey suggested that persons of other religions (e.g., Taoists, Buddhists, Muslims, and even atheists like the philosopher Spinoza) might have experienced similar kinds of transformations.

> The way in which the experience operated, its function, determines its religious value. If the reorientation actually occurs, it, and the sense of the security and stability accompanying it, are forces on their own account. It takes place in different persons in a multitude of ways. (Dewey, 1934, p. 14)

While religions claim to have this effect of reorientation and change of will, Dewey proposed that "whenever this change takes place there is a definitely religious attitude.... When it occurs, from whatever cause and by whatever means, there is a religious outlook and function" (p. 17). Unlike religion itself, this kind of attitude is not bounded or tied to a particular way of life or specific institution; rather, it can be much broader and can even be expressed through art, science, or good citizenship.

For Dewey, this religious attitude promotes understanding and knowledge based upon continuous and rigorous inquiry. Such an attitude would be different from one that is limited in scope and dependent upon dogma or a specific interpretation of doctrine.

Iranian writer Azar Nafisi (2005) exemplified this distinction between religion and religious attitude as she recalled a scene from Mark Twain's *Huckleberry Finn*. In this scene, the young Huck Finn contemplates what to do about his friend Jim, a runaway slave:

> Huck asks himself whether he should give Jim up or not. Huck was told in Sunday School that people who let slaves go free go to "everlasting fire." But then, Huck says he imagines he and Jim in "the day and nighttime, sometimes moonlight, sometimes storms, and we afloating along, talking and singing and laughing." Huck remembers Jim and their friendship and warmth. He imagines Jim not as a slave but as a human being and he decides that, "alright then, I'll go to hell."

Nafisi explained how this story relates to her own experiences with university students in Tehran.

> What Huck rejects is not religion but an attitude of self-righteousness and inflexibility. I remember this particular scene out of *Huck Finn* so vividly today, because I associate it with a difficult time in my own life. In the early 1980s when I taught at the University of Tehran, I, like many others, was expelled. I was very surprised to discover that my staunchest allies were two students who were very active at the University's powerful Muslim Students' Association. These young men and I had engaged in very passionate and heated arguments. I had fiercely opposed their ideological stances. But that didn't stop them from defending me. When I ran into one of them after my expulsion, I thanked him for his support. "We are not as rigid as you imagine us to be, Professor Nafisi," he responded. "Remember your own lectures on

Huck Finn? Let's just say, he is not the only one who can risk going to hell!"

The religious attitude that Dewey distinguished is evident in Huckleberry Finn's rejection of an attitude of self-righteousness, as noted by Professor Nafisi. But more powerfully, it is learned and practiced by her Iranian students as they defended her right to teach. As Dewey said, it is an attitude that promotes understanding through knowledge.

THE SACRED AND THE HOLY

Fasching et al. (2011) offered another way to consider this kind of transcendent religious attitude. The distinction between religion and the religious is evident in what is held to be *sacred* in contrast with what is considered *holy*. *Sacred* refers to an ordering of society in terms of morality, that is, knowing what ought to be done and is obligatory. In early tribal societies, this meant honoring the gods or spirits to ensure that goodness would prevail. In contemporary times, the notion of sacred reflects what we hold important and cherish about our society.

As such, our modern secular society might exhibit a sacred morality in responding to actions. If the American flag is burned or a cross is desecrated, then we as Americans might find those acts to be offensive. While flag burning is clearly a political act and the other is more obviously tied to the Christian religion, both are examples of objects held to be sacred and honored in our country. Similarly Muslims were outraged in 2005 when a Danish newspaper printed cartoons depicting their Prophet Muhammed as a terrorist. Publishing these cartoons represented an act viewed as sacrilegious and disrespectful to Muslims worldwide.

Contrasting with the sacred, the experience of the *holy* encourages us to consider wholeness rather than right versus wrong. Fasching et al. (2011) proposed:

> The task of an ethic of the holy is not to eliminate the morality of society, but to transform it by breaking down the divisions between the sacred and profane through narratives of hospitality to the stranger, which affirm the human dignity of precisely those who do not share one's identity and one's stories. (p. 17)

This is essentially the religious attitude that Dewey identified, one that draws from the diversity and richness of having a pluralistic society. It enables questioning and encourages us to deconstruct what we hold to be obligatory. This kind of critique advances societal thinking and promotes human dignity.

> While a sacred society is founded on a shared set of answers which belong to the finite world of "the way things are," a holy community is

founded on experiences of openness to the infinite . . . seeing and acting
on new possibilities. (Fasching et al., 2011, p. 18)

As the sacred and the holy propose different ways to think about our
traditions and beliefs, we advocate not choosing one over the other. Rather, reflect upon what is sacred and needing to be preserved in our society.
What do we hold to be important, and why? Are these values and beliefs
shared, and by whom? As well, consider what is deemed holy, that
which brings us together as a community. What are the ways to think
about who we are as a people that can unite rather than divide us? What
traditions and beliefs emphasize our collective unity rather than our deep
divisions? Both notions of the sacred and the holy can be useful in thinking through what we believe and value individually and collectively.

ADMINISTRATIVE WORK

In our work as school administrators, regardless of our religious traditions and beliefs, we must honor the freedoms permitted by our democratic society. Legally, we are obligated to abide by the U.S. Constitution
as interpreted by the Supreme Court. Religious beliefs are a private matter, and as such, we respect the free choice of individuals to profess their
faith in whatever way they choose.

Different from times past when one was born into a particular faith
because of one's family background (e.g., when to be Irish meant to be
Catholic), individuals today are much freer to decide their religious values, beliefs, and practices based on their own volition. They may be
raised in one faith tradition, convert to another as adults, and partner
with someone of yet another religious orientation. There are more choices
to believe and practice freely in our American society.

Perhaps because of this freedom to choose, individuals hold more
steadfastly to their convictions. According to Strike et al. (1998),

> [r]eligious convictions are often central to people's conception of who
> they are and what their fundamental duties and obligations are. To
> treat religious convictions as objects of potential public interest is to
> open a path for doing great violence to individuals. We treat religious
> belief and practice as largely a private matter not so much because
> these things have no public consequences, but because they have such
> profound personal consequences. (p. 36)

We also recognize that we are members of a civil society that accommo-
dates diversity and differences. There is no singular religious institution
fundamental to our social order and organization; rather, there are varied
social institutions formed for educational, political, economic, philanthropic, and scientific purposes that occur independently of any religion

and influence our actions. This was noted in chapter 2 as we wrote of ethical tensions created by our diverse affiliations and memberships.

Our work as educational leaders directs us to honor individuals' values and beliefs while teaching tolerance and accommodating diverse perspectives. Schools can be places where youngsters learn about different histories, cultures, religious beliefs, and values. They can also be places for discussion and debate where students learn to respect as well as critique alternative perspectives. We believe that students should have the opportunity to think for themselves about what is just and right, good and caring. They need to develop their capacity to reflect upon their views, defend their positions, and even change their minds.

By the same token, schools need to respect a student's right to disagree, as Strike et al. (1998) stated in the following example. Suppose a student's religion teaches that homosexuality is a sin.

> Schools might explain . . . that homosexuals are entitled to equal rights regardless of whether homosexuality is a sin. But schools need not insist that these students view homosexuality as merely an alternative lifestyle. (p. 139)

We would strengthen this statement by referring to Dewey's definition of democracy. No person, whether he or she agrees or disagrees with another, has the right to limit the potential of another. In other words, schools, workplaces, and other public institutions must be able to foster the growth of all of their members, whether conservative Christian or gay student. Leaders must be cognizant of this reality in order to establish equitable spaces.

Administrative work in any public sphere involves an ethic of democratic leadership. It requires human intelligence, which Dewey (1934) calls "ardor in behalf of light shining into the murky places of social existence, and as zeal for its refreshing and purifying effect" (p. 79). Intelligence directed toward justice and security, he says, is evident in human nature. "Human beings have impulses toward affection, compassion and justice, equality and freedom. It remains to weld all these things together" (p. 81).

SUMMARY

In this chapter, we explored how our religious views might influence the antecedent beliefs that form our decisions. Beginning with a definition of religion and how it has evolved as societies have diversified, we considered how our religious traditions inform our moral–ethical choices. These traditions provide direction for what we deem to be a good person, what is right action, and what defines a moral–ethical society.

We also considered religious freedom as a guaranteed right of American citizenship that should be protected within our schools. Beyond this legal dimension, Dewey's notion of religious attitude enables us to be more open to inquiry. As well, the distinction between the sacred and the holy can be used to think through what we value and believe for living with others. We reflected upon the work expected of administrators who need to honor religious freedom while accommodating multiple perspectives.

FOUR

Feminist Ethics and Ecofeminism

In our increasingly global society, we recognize that differing sociocultural groups have contrasting philosophies about what makes for right action and desirable outcomes. In the previous chapters, we identified various sources of ethical tension and diverse religious traditions that create conflicts as individuals and groups live together.

Nowhere is such conflict more evident than in our public schools. Students bring their unique sociocultural backgrounds—backgrounds as diverse as a first-generation Vietnamese immigrant living in a Minnesota suburb, an African American Methodist who plays soccer with an Indian American Sikh, or a gifted young Lithuanian violinist with attention deficit disorder—into our public schools and under our sphere of influence.

These students do not check their diversity at the school door, nor do they leave behind their family backgrounds and ethnic origins. Neither do they bring only part of who they are, leaving their special talents, abilities, and challenges behind. As one educator reminded us, "The youngsters who come to our schools bring the very best of themselves."

Diversity is not only a consideration for schools. As a country the United States has experienced unprecedented racial–ethnic diversification that many demographers believe will result in a white minority by 2050. Indeed, this was at play in our 2012 presidential elections. The need to ensure equitable opportunities, procedures, and standards, while expected in public schools, has now become evident in social, political, and economic arenas as well.

As democratic leaders, our work is twofold. First, we are charged with serving all of our constituents fairly, equitably, and respectfully. That involves recognizing the individual differences and sociocultural backgrounds that they bring. It is about being open to others who might be

49

different from us and providing educational, social, political, and other options for everyone.

A second aim of our work as leaders is to honor the shared values and beliefs that unify us as a democratic society. It means preparing our students to become successful and productive citizens, valued for their contributions and capable of working together, and then ensuring that our citizens are able to enjoy equitable opportunities for a good life. We propose that these two aims are highly related to becoming effective, democratic leaders who make ethical judgments in diverse settings.

To address the tasks of leadership outlined above, we offer a theoretical lens—feminism—that has us look particularly at the differences that women bring to making ethical choices. Our rationale for presenting this perspective is to suggest how a critical theory can frame ethical issues and provide alternative yet equally valid ways to resolve and reconcile conflicts. It is especially useful because it offers a means for questioning and critiquing what we take for granted and encourages the direction of actions toward ethical deliberation.

We first define feminism and its three tenets. By focusing on areas in which feminism has been applied, we suggest ways to think about ethical decision making, and specifically consider school administrative work from a feminist perspective. Like all theories, feminism has its limitations, and these are also discussed. In concluding, we propose a move beyond the limitations of the theory with a more comprehensive version of feminism as it can be applied to ethical leadership.

DEFINITION OF FEMINISM

The term *feminism*, according to Houston (1996), refers broadly to the feminist theory and social movement that advocate for creating a society where women can live full, self-determined lives. Historian Joan Kelly characterized feminism as having three tenets:

> (1) a deliberate and conscious opposition to male defamation and mistreatment of women; (2) a belief that the sexes are culturally and not just biologically formed, that women are a social group shaped by male notions of their sex; and (3) a desire for a conception of humanity that recognizes women as fully human. (Kelly as referenced in Houston, 1996, p. 215)

The first tenet of feminism echoes the struggle for women's rights. The "first wave" in the struggle was the women's suffrage movement, which in the United States can be traced back to Elizabeth Cady Stanton's declaration of women's rights at the Seneca Falls Convention in 1848. It would be another seventy-two years before American women actually did attain voting rights in 1920. Contrastingly, these full rights of citizenship were accorded to white men in the eighteenth century during the American Revolution.

A "second wave" in the struggle occurred in the 1960s, with attention drawn to the civil rights of women, minorities, and marginalized peoples. Major sociopolitical institutions like the government, economy, and educational systems were criticized, as were social conventions such as marriage, family, and sexuality.

This evolution of the feminist movement from the 1960s into the 1980s relates to the second tenet, a critique that the "sexes are culturally, and not just biologically formed" (Houston, 1996, p. 215). The concept of "gender" emerged as distinct from biological sexuality. That is, to be a woman was not the same as to be female; *woman* refers to one's social, cultural, and political positioning within a given society within a specific time period, whereas *female* simply distinguishes one from being *male*.

As feminism evolved, formulating the concept of gender has revealed new aspects of male dominance in areas never before acknowledged. Also, social factors, such as one's class, race, ethnicity, sexual orientation, and age, were seen as determinants of how one's gender was regarded. This acknowledgment pushed feminists to consider the multiple ways that social and cultural factors have confounded women's experiences and maintained structures of domination.

The third tenet of feminism advocates for women being fully recognized as fellow human beings. The National Organization for Women (NOW) expressed this tenet in seeking "full equality for women in a truly equal partnership with men." Women were viewed as subordinates to men in most social spheres so the organization advocated change in the workplace, home, and civic circles. Later with greater political activism, NOW professed bolder goals of "women's liberation" and campaigned for legal and financial equality, equal work opportunity, and other emancipatory demands (Delmar, 2001). Beyond American borders, NOW currently promotes issues of human rights and dignity to end the domination of women worldwide.

Significant strides in the feminist movement have been made in our country. In the political arena, these include legislating for affirmative action, passing the Equal Rights Amendment in Congress, and electing more women politicians. In economics, strides have been made in closing the wage gap between men and women and in providing more professional avenues of employment for women. Certain social mores, such as recognizing lesbian and gay relationships, have been liberalized.

Focusing on violence against women, advocates have raised awareness of domestic violence and the prevalence of sexual harassment of girls. Others have worked in health and human services to provide essential health care for women, shelters for battered women and families, and twenty-four-hour rape crisis centers. Some advocates have lobbied for self-determination through affirming abortion rights for women and teens. Still others have targeted pornography and violence resulting from the denigration of women in the media.

Feminists in the United States have linked with those in Third World, as well as developed, nations to promote international resolutions for human dignity. Activists have worked to establish fair wages and to ensure educational opportunities for women. The brutal repression of women was evident in the 2012 case of Malala Yousafzai, a fourteen-year-old girl shot in the head by a Taliban gunman while she was riding home on a school bus. Her "crime" was advocating for the education of Pakistani girls like herself. Her amazing recovery has been seen as a beacon of hope to those seeking to end the violence against women.

FEMINISM APPLIED TO SCHOOL LEADERSHIP

In focusing on gender inequities, feminist scholarship in education has attempted to uncover and dislodge white male-dominated frameworks within institutions, work life, and social structures. Marshall (1997) suggested that feminist and critical theories offer useful lenses for looking at schools and asking the following kinds of questions: Why do social class, race–ethnicity, and gender inequities persist in this school or system? Do instructional practices reinforce stereotypes of masculinity and femininity? Are white male administrators preferred over women and minorities? Do leaders value organizational efficiency over relationships and caregiving?

> There is room for decades of policy research which asks first, how does this policy or structure exclude certain publics (subordinate nationalities, religions, women, the urban poor, the working class, homosexuals), then asks, what political arrangements support policies and structures that devalue alternative perspectives, that reinforce gender, ethnic/race and class inequities, and asks, who benefits from these arrangements, and finally, what are possible ways to restructure power dynamics and political arrangements to address issues of social justice. (Marshall, 1997, p. 2)

Such scholarship can be categorized into three complementary yet distinctive areas of study, as depicted in Table 4.1. The first area involves work within the system. The assumption is that equity will be achieved when barriers to gender are eliminated and when women attain positions of power and influence within the existing system. Examples are policies like Affirmative Action, the Equal Rights Amendment, and Title IX. A limitation of this perspective is that those who are currently in power have essentially created the sexism and racism that is denigrating others. Moreover, it might be naive to expect that the powerful would willingly change the status quo, yielding to others who have little or no power.

A second area of study reflects the view that women's ways of knowing and taking action are fundamentally different from those of men. In her groundbreaking book *In a Different Voice*, psychologist Carol Gilligan (1982) provided empirical evidence to support a feminist revision of moral development.

Human development theory had been founded on the masculine myth of the hero's journey in which male experiences set the standard. Gilligan's mentor Lawrence Kohlberg conducted a longitudinal study of eighty-four men from childhood to adulthood. On the basis of the study, he proposed a model of six developmental stages of moral judgment whereby individuals were thought to evolve from pre-conventional to mature responses to ethical problems. On Kohlberg's scale, women were usually judged to be less ethically mature than men because of their responses.

However, in studying eleven-year-old boys and girls, Gilligan found that the girls saw the ethical problem differently than the boys did. For the girls, the challenge was to sustain relationships, not necessarily to ensure justice, as was the case for the boys. Gilligan concluded that wom-

Table 4.1.   Feminist Areas of Study

Area of Study	Focus	Assumptions	Examples	Limitations
Equity	More equitable treatment and opportunities within established systems.	When barriers based upon gender are broken down, then equity will be achieved.	Affirmative action, equal rights, Title IX nondiscrimination policies.	Assumes that those who hold power are responsible for current systems' change.
Women's ways of knowing	Women's experience of their world is different from men's and should be honored.	By honoring women's ways of knowing, women become full partners in any endeavor.	Gilligan's development of an ethic of care was different from but as viable as an ethic of justice.	Can be interpreted as essentialist, universal, and enduring.
Power	Deconstruction of power relationships, inequitable structures, rules, patterns, and language.	For true equity to be achieved, systems must be redesigned. Rules and patterns must be established to balance power.	Ferguson's study of how bureaucracies control and stifle women.	Power relationships are often embedded in culture and norms and thus are difficult to detect.

en were not less morally developed; rather, they chose to employ care for and sensitivity to the needs of others when making ethical decisions.

This research points toward the need to question fundamental assumptions of similarity and difference between the genders. Unlike men, women do not necessarily follow similar patterns, nor should they be deemed less or inferior but merely different.

Power is the third area of study in which feminism identifies aspects of the purposes and processes within an organization or system that create and maintain gender inequities. Ferguson (1984) identified ways in which structures, rules, language, and patterns of domination in bureaucracies serve to control women, stifling their alternative ways of talking, valuing, and living their lives. Boldly, she advocated for a nonbureaucratic approach to organizations, "conceiving the individual and the collective that reflects the care taking and nurturant experiences embedded in women's role" (Ferguson, 1984, p. x).

As feminist scholars pursue this research, they might consider the informal as well as the formal mechanisms of sexism, an organization's historical precedence for male domination, and value-laden assumptions constraining minority or nondominant views. Unfortunately, because power relations within organizations and systems can be embedded and nested, decoupling power and gender to decipher inequities may be challenging.

ADMINISTRATIVE WORK FROM A FEMINIST PERSPECTIVE

In the early development of school administration, John Franklin Brown (1909) published what became a classic text for high school principals titled *The American High School*. Regarding the importance of gender among the qualifications for principalship, Brown wrote,

> Generally speaking, men make better principals than women, especially in large schools. They are stronger physically; they possess more executive ability; they are more likely to command the confidence of male citizens; they are more judicial in mind; they are more sure to seize upon the essential merits of a question; they are less likely to look at things from a personal point of view; they are likely to be better supported by subordinates; and simply because they are men, they are more likely to command fully the respect and confidence of boys. (pp. 241–242)

Nearly a hundred years later, the perception remains that men make better leaders than women, especially at the secondary school level, for the same reasons given by Brown in the early twentieth century. Men are viewed as physically stronger, appear to be more rational and objective, and have the ability to "rally the troops" toward action, especially in handling the rowdy and belligerent.

From a feminist perspective, we challenge such a perception and question whether it is based exclusively upon men's experiences. As researchers (Belenky, Clinchy, Goldberger, & Tarule, 1986; Ferguson, 1984; Gilligan, 1982) have done, we consider whether there might be perceived differences between women and men because of differing social upbringings and culture. Do men and women make decisions differently? Should women's decision making be measured against men's? Are women's ways of knowing and deciding equally worthy of consideration? If so, then why have their voices been stifled or silenced? How might we be more inclusive of their experiences?

The 2012 election resulted in more women into the federal legislative branch. The presence of twenty women senators means that more will chair legislative committees, introduce legislation, and raise human rights concerns more readily.

For example, Senators Kirsten Gillibrand, Barbara Boxer, and other legislators prompted a critical look at the issue of rape and sexual assaults occurring in the military. The Senate Armed Services subcommittee heard from victims long silenced because of their military service. Of the estimated 19,000 incidents of sexual assault occurring in 2010 alone, only 13.5 percent had been reported, and an even smaller percentage, 191 cases in all, resulted in convictions. Gillibrand and fellow senators have brought military officials in for questioning about these disturbing findings (Green, 2013).

In public education, there is more support for appointing women to lead schools and school districts. In terms of experience, women continue to dominate the field of teaching and thus bring more years of classroom experience to the task of being instructional leaders. They also have entered graduate programs in greater numbers for professional certification and advanced degrees. More women are serving as elementary school principals than ever before. In sum, women bring teaching experience, graduate education, and administrative preparation to demonstrate their competence for holding administrative positions at the secondary and system levels.

But it is not sufficient to increase the numbers of women in administrative positions and eliminate the barriers that prevent women from accessing positions of power and influence. A feminist perspective on administrative work demands that equal consideration be given to values traditionally deemed "feminine," such as caregiving, nurturance, relationship development, and community building. Rather than dismissing these values as subjective and personalized, a feminist perspective honors the importance of caregiving within educational settings, challenging all who serve as administrators to draw upon their emotions as well as intellect to understand student needs (Noddings, 1992).

In *The Least of These*, a fictional account of an urban elementary school principal, Mary Van Cleave (1994) writes about placing priority on the

needs of children. Rather than addressing declining test scores by remediation or by fine-tuning the curriculum, she believes that the first job of
teachers should be the children. She writes of this from the perspective of
the principal, Marilyn Wallace:

> We have some other things to do first. We need to make the children as
> secure as we can. We need to see who they are—what they like and
> don't like, what their strengths are. Let's give them a school where they
> can get their hands on things, get involved in projects that answer the
> questions they have about their world. Let's let them talk to us and to
> each other. I don't care about the test scores. I really don't care. What
> matters is that the children have a school where they feel safe and
> secure and loved, where they feel as if they have something to contrib-
> ute, where they feel their own worth. If we can work together to create
> that kind of environment, they'll learn everything we want them to
> learn—and more. (Van Cleave, 1994, p. 15)

An administrator who holds a feminist perspective will raise issues about
how a school privileges some and oppresses others. Not only is gender
discrimination considered, but class, race–ethnicity, age, sexual orientation, and other means of marginalizing youngsters are uncovered.

- Are there ways in which the school categorizes, stereotypes, and
  thereby excludes certain individuals or groups from equal access,
  open enrollment, and free participation?
- How are teachers and staff supported in understanding the different sociocultural groups within the school?
- Is there a mentality about assimilating and socializing all youngsters in the same way throughout the American public education
  system?
- What are the success rates and achievements among different
  groups of students?
- Do certain groups require assistance or remediation? If so, is there a
  "blame-the-victim" approach to providing that assistance?
- To what extent does the school encourage alternative instructional
  practices that might be culturally sensitive?

School administrators can be key in promoting equal opportunity and
equitable treatment that enable students to succeed despite the challenges of poverty, second-language learning, and special needs.

LIMITATIONS OF A FEMINIST PERSPECTIVE

Because feminism evolved from acknowledging women's perspectives, a
fundamental limitation is that the perspective might be viewed strictly as
"women's work" and be exclusively reserved for only women to under-
take. Among the sharpest critics of feminism have been those who hold

traditional views of the role of women as homemakers and primary care-givers in the private domain. They argue for retaining this exclusivity. By contrast, feminists advocate that women's worlds should not be limited or bounded within the private domain. Women's contributions in social, economic, and political arenas attest to doing so.

A second limitation is that feminism tends to view women collective-ly, making their perspective essentialized. Belenky et al. (1986) proposed that women's ways of acquiring and organizing knowledge were funda-mentally different from men's. Yet as was noted earlier, not all women's experiences and ways of knowing are necessarily similar.

Specifically, women of color and on the margins, such as lesbians, Jewish women, Native American women, and older women, have felt that their lived experiences as women and minorities are not reflected in the feminist discourse. While white women might be victims of one sys-tem of domination because of their gender, they have remained agents of domination because of their "whiteness." This criticism has demanded that feminists reconsider whose perspectives are being reflected and what other social factors might confound women's experiences.

A counterargument can be drawn from postmodern thinkers like Richard Rorty, who suggests that we recognize and celebrate the multi-plicity of viewpoints.

> Constructing gender is a process, not an answer. In using a postmod-ernist approach, we open the possibility of theorizing gender in hereto-fore unimagined ways. Postmodernism allows us to see that as observ-ers of gender we are also its creators. (Hare-Mustin & Marecek, 2001, p. 102)

A feminist perspective çan become an evolving viewpoint that honors difference—female–male, young–old, white–nonwhite, gay–straight—and that attempts to be inclusive rather than exclusive in its orientation. Christian ecofeminist Rosemary Ruether (1992) proposed that "what unites us in a common struggle and social vision is far more important than the differences that distinguish us" (p. xix).

A third limitation of feminism arises from trying to be all things to everyone, accommodating the depth and breadth of women's experi-ences. A challenge has been to define a theoretical stance that places women at the center and yet includes the varied life experiences of mar-ginalized women and minorities. Though most advocates direct their ef-forts against gender oppression, some criticize a feminism that gener-alizes from white, middle-class women's experiences.

> The problem of how to create feminist theory that reflects the reality of women and avoids a monolithic view of women remains unresolved. The task is both to maintain the category women and at the same time embrace the differences within this category. (Houston, 1996, p. 218)

As with many applications of theory, there is a divide between feminist theory and how it is practiced, and proponents push for more pragmatic action to replace academic theorizing. "Feminist activists point out that re-describing and creating new meaning in theory is not enough to stop battering, promote reproductive freedom, or end child abuse" (Houston, 1996, p. 218).

For some, the ultimate end of feminism is the total eradication of domination and oppression. According to bell hooks (1984),

> Feminism is a commitment to eradicating the ideology of domination that permeates Western culture on various levels—sex, race, class to name a few—and a commitment to reorganizing . . . society, so that the self development of people can take precedence over imperialism, economic expansion and material desires. (as quoted in Houston, 1996, p. 217)

Given the scope of the problem and the need for taking action, it might be wise to take Ruether's (1992) advice that we hold a long-term view into the future:

> Our revolution is not just for us, but for our children, for the generations of living beings to come. What we can do is to plant a seed, nurture a seed-bearing plant here and there, and hope for a harvest that goes beyond the limits of our powers and the span of our lives. (pp. 273–274)

MOVING TOWARD ECOFEMINISM

A leader who seeks a viable and sustaining vision for the future needs to include all voices, those of women as well as men, those of different classes, racial--ethnicities, sexual orientations, religious diversities, and more. To do so, Fasching et al. (2011) proposed moving beyond feminism and its limitations toward a combination of ecology and feminism, called *ecofeminism*.

The authors begin with the assumption that each life exists within a complex social ecology consisting of one's family, friendships, work life, associations, and civic and religious communities. Each of these spheres forms a social–institutional context, which holds an implicit set of expectations, values, and beliefs that make up its morality. A school administrator could be a daughter, spouse, painter, Rotarian, golfer, and Catholic. All of these different social contexts contribute to an understanding of good and evil, right and wrong, and positive and negative.

Each social context may have a set of implicit expectations about what makes a good person, be it a dutiful daughter, a loving parent, or an effective school administrator. We maintain a multiplicity of personalities that address our diverse social contexts.

I am a different person with my family than I am with my boss, and different still with my friends, and so on. Each of the social environments we enter—work, family, friendship, voluntary associations, political movements, religious communities, etc.—require us to be a different person. And every one of the social roles we embrace in constructing our social identities has a story or complex of stories attached to it, which we consciously or unconsciously absorb. (Fasching et al., 2011, p. 333)

In leading an ethical life, the challenge is to fulfill the myriad of expectations placed upon us in each context. Parents know this challenge when they are forced to juggle work responsibilities and a sick child. The stress can be even greater with a long-term illness of a child or family member. It is further compounded when one is responsible for the well-being of numerous others as school administrators caring for students, teachers, and staff.

According to Fasching et al. (2011), maintaining these multiplicities is possible through our capacity to "double." This process involves alienating our own selves, what the authors call "secondary doubling." It can be useful, as we are able to see our actions objectively and reflect upon them.

But secondary doubling can be problematic when we are not personally connected with what we do. In bureaucratic organizations like school systems, we are often compartmentalized within roles and responsibilities. Someone at the top decides to take a particular action directed toward a particular end. Without necessarily questioning the decision, administrators follow orders as directed. In ordinary circumstances, such action may be considered routine, but at its extremes, the "secondary doubling" can alienate us from our best ethical behavior.

Parker Palmer (2004) illustrated this in a story about a government bureaucrat who was experiencing painful conflicts between his values and power politics. It happened at a retreat that Palmer led in Washington, DC.

One participant had worked for a decade in the U.S. Department of Agriculture, after farming for twenty-five years in northeastern Iowa. On his desk at that moment was a proposal related to the preservation of midwestern topsoil, which is being depleted at a rapid rate by agribusiness practices that value short term profits over the well-being of the earth. His "farmer's heart," he kept saying, knew how the proposal should be handled. But his political instincts warned him that following his heart would result in serious trouble, not least with his immediate superior.

On the last morning of our gathering, the man from Agriculture, looking bleary-eyed, told us that it had become clear to him during a sleepless night that he needed to return to his office and follow his farmer's heart.

> After a thoughtful silence, someone asked him, "How will you deal with your boss, given his opposition to what you intend to do?"
>
> "It won't be easy," replied this farmer-turned-bureaucrat. "But during this retreat, I've remembered something important: I don't report to my boss. I report to the land." (pp. 18–19)

Palmer cautioned that he did not know whether the man did return to work and do as he resolved, but it was clear that he had validated what was most important to him. He tried to bring together his multiple selves, that of farmer, bureaucrat, citizen, and caretaker of the earth.

With ecofeminism, Fasching et al. (2011) proposed that we can attend to these multiple moral identities within our diverse social contexts. It validates the importance of diversity and reminds us that the greater the complexity present in life, the more likely is survival, a lesson learned from evolution.

> The more complexity there is in our social life (i.e., the more roles we must play in various social/institutional contexts), the more sensitive and life-sustaining our conscience will be. And conversely, the less complex and more simplified our social ecology becomes, the less sensitive and life-sustaining our conscience will be. (p. 334)

Another way of looking at ecofeminism is through what Margaret Urban Walker (1998) called "the structure of our responsibilities. . . . Specific moral claims on us arise from our contact or relationship with others whose interests are vulnerable to our actions and choices" (p. 107). Walker suggested applying an ethic of care but cautioned that women need to rise above the bottomless pit of self-sacrifice and nurturing that denies their own personal integrity.

Also, an ethic of personal integrity that denies empathy for others is equally unacceptable. Walker stated the two aspects, care and integrity, might guide us into "the right relations with morality's guiding and constraining force within those lives" (Walker, 1998, p. 108).

How might we accomplish such a balance? Virginia Held (1993) observed,

> Since feminist approaches to morality are suspicious of rather than eager to offer highly abstract theories and simple principles, they are more likely to emphasize methods of moral inquiry and processes of moral improvement than to propound finished, comprehensive theories. (p. 219)

Consider a young man who reflected upon his work as a newly appointed elementary school principal. "You know, I recently became a dad, and it's changed how I think about my work. I mean, I wonder, what if this kid were my kid? How would I feel? I try to think about the parents' perspective more than ever before." In theory, the needs of a specific child should be cared about, but by turning inquiry on such care in a concrete way, this principal has moved beyond an abstract theory of care to one that maintains his own personal integrity while making the concept more real. It is a theory that Charlene Haddock Seigfried (1996) characterized as "inquiry directed toward changing situations, preeminently social situations, which always include human participants" (p. 263).

Every social–institutional context confronts us with genuine ethical obligations toward others. It is possible to cultivate the awareness necessary to assume more than one identification and to see the world through more than one social context. This ecology of conscience is a relational–ecological model of justice, care, and personal integrity whereby the self is not set apart from others but moves in multiple social roles and across multiple contexts. Fasching et al. (2011) stated

> The more complexity there is, the more strangers enter into our life and the broader and more inclusive our ethical consciousness becomes. The ethical life requires more than just taking care of one's friends; it demands hospitality to the stranger (both human and non-human). (p. 336)

SUMMARY

By challenging taken-for-granted ways of thinking, feminism presents us with an alternative perspective that informs our moral–ethical decisions in a way different from an ethic of justice and moral development. In this chapter, we described feminist ethics and its fundamental tenets as applied in three areas of study—equity, women's ways of knowing, and power. There are various ways that feminism might inform our thinking as leaders in society at large and specifically as school administrators.

Yet we can recognize some of its limitations—as women's work, as essentialist, and as too theoretical. To move beyond these limitations, we offered the more encompassing perspective of ecofeminism that recognizes the multiple contexts in which we live and work. This is a model of critique that is highly appropriate for engaging in democratic leadership.

FIVE

Leadership for Social Justice

Sharon Radd, Ed.D., St. Catherine University

Taking a stand to right the inequalities of class, race, gender, and other diversities is the essential work of a leader with a social justice agenda. However, more needs to be understood about this responsibility, especially in light of the ethical tensions that might be present in doing the work. The aim of this chapter is to provide a conceptual frame and practical application for that understanding.

As in previous chapters, we begin by defining the challenge for leaders embarking on a social justice agenda and the preparation necessary to meet the challenge. For the school leader who aims to use effective, inclusive, and meaningful approaches, we suggest three key theoretical lenses for social justice. Moving toward a pragmatic method to ethical decision making, we suggest some internal barriers and considerations in skillfully and effectively leading. We conclude by foreshadowing the next chapter on Dewey's approach to democratic and ethical leadership.

DEFINITION OF SOCIAL JUSTICE LEADERSHIP

While school administrators are challenged to provide for equity and excellence in the delivery of public education for all youngsters, their task is further complicated by increasing demographic diversity in our student population, inequities among different groups that negatively impact underserved impoverished areas, and achievement gaps notably between majority and minority students (Larson & Murtadha, 2002; Marshall & Oliva, 2010; Riehl, 2000; Theoharis, 2007). According to Pounder, Reitzug, and Young (2002),

> Schools across our nation in districts large and small with different
> resources and different student populations are failing to educate, fail-
> ing to nurture, failing to develop, failing to protect, and failing to in-
> clude all students. . . . [T]he students who are affected most are typical-
> ly from marginalized groups (e.g., students of color, students with dis-
> abilities, low-income students, girls, and gay/lesbian students). (p. 271)

Such failings occur in some places in our country but not all; there are
many schools and school districts that have made important strides in
educating all children well. Darling-Hammond (2010) postulated that the
successes of these schools relate to having created a teaching and learning
system that is based upon a strong, equitable, and excellent public education delivered to all students.

> Such a system not only prepares all teachers and school leaders well for
> the challenging work they are asked to do, but it ensures that schools
> are organized to support both student and teacher learning, and that
> standards, curriculum, and assessments that guide their work encour-
> age the kind of knowledge and abilities needed in the 21st century. (p.
> 26)

Creating and sustaining such a system is the moral, ethical, and democratic challenge of leaders committed to a vision of social justice in which
equity and excellence are provided for all students of a diverse and inclusive American society.

PREPARING SOCIAL JUSTICE LEADERS

To meet this challenge, school leaders must recognize the inequities
among different groups, commit to sustained systemic educational re-
forms, and work with all stakeholders to address social justice issues
effectively (Bogotch, 2002, 2005; Brown, 2004; Capper, Theoharis, & Sebastian, 2006; Dantley & Tillman, 2010; Larson & Murtadha, 2002; Marshall & Oliva, 2010; Scheurich & Skrla, 2003; Theoharis, 2007).

McKenzie et al. (2008) identified that the school leader's work is to
create an educational setting directed at raising student achievement,
narrowing the gaps, and preparing a knowledgeable citizenry, all within
a heterogeneous yet inclusive school. These goals are achievable only
through dedicated action and a commitment toward just and equitable
education for all children served in a public school.

Currently, most American university-based administrator preparation
programs do not adequately prepare school leaders to effectively address
these complex challenges (Darling-Hammond, LaPointe, Meyerson, Orr,
& Cohen, 2009; Howley, Andrianaivo, & Perry, 2005; Levine, 2005;
Spring, 2001).

Using survey data from eighteen of the sixty-two universities affiliated with the University Council for Educational Administration (UCEA),

Hawley and James (2010) identified that coursework on issues related to diversity most often occurs in a single course that focuses on the sociopolitical and sociocultural context and consequences of inequality. These courses and their affiliated programs give little attention to the everyday issues of diversity that arise in classrooms and schools and how leaders might effectively address them.

In a review of seven states' standards, Cambron-McCabe (2010) found that while most programs gave "considerable attention to formulating detailed, comprehensive standards for administrative licensure," those same programs could not identify the specific aspects of their standards related to social justice (p. 37). In addition to knowledge about policies that address social justice issues (e.g., equity, equal opportunity, provisions for those with diverse needs), licensure and preparation programs need to go further to foster the skills and know-how to effectively lead for social justice.

Scholars vary considerably in their recommendations for how this might be done. Several (Cambron-McCabe & McCarthy, 2005; Rusch, 2004; Theoharis, 2007) advocate for the need to probe and question one's personal value-laden assumptions and, by doing so, delve into critical inquiry related to what is being taught, by whom, and toward what end. Feldman and Tyson (2007) contended that an understanding of topics such as anti-bias education, critical pedagogy, multicultural education, and whiteness studies is essential to effective social justice leadership.

Furman (2012) proposed going beyond the rhetoric of social justice principles to encourage praxis (i.e., reflection as well as action), beginning with the personal and interpersonal and extending toward the communal, systemic, and ecological. Such praxis requires building a leader's skills to take transformative action and engagement.

Moreover, leaders will need to navigate the inherent tension between "the world as it is" and "the world as it should be." Do we teach disenfranchised students the means to get ahead in the current system, knowing that it retains the mechanisms that create and maintain inequality? Or do we teach students to create a different world, knowing that without certain forms of power and capital, they may not be able to influence the future? We propose that leaders advocating for social justice stay in the thick of that tension by recognizing the inequities perpetuated within the social, political, and economic realms of today's world while navigating with everyone—students, families, teachers, and community—headed toward a different future.

THREE THEORETICAL LENSES

The work of social justice is among the most challenging work that any leader can take on. It requires an active equity lens, the discernment to envision meaningful change, and the ability to act skillfully to engage others in that change. In this section we present three theoretical frames that undergird the philosophical center from which one can initiate effective social justice. Later in the chapter, we describe such action, but first we present three key components of a social justice orientation: (a) transformative learning, (b) critical theory, and (c) organizational and social change.

TRANSFORMATIVE LEARNING

Developed as a "theory in progress" by Mezirow (2000), this frame begins with the understanding that early life experiences, socialization, and relations form an individual's fundamental ways of seeing the world. Transformation theory explores how one negotiates and refines those original understandings of the world to become an agent of one's own meaning making rather than a product and agent of one's upbringing and early social context.

The term *frames of reference* refers to one's underlying mental schema that fundamentally shape one's meaning making of every aspect of the world. Powerful and persistent forces in one's thinking can go largely unnoticed but their influence can be profound. Mezirow (2000) wrote:

> Our values and sense of self are anchored in our frames of reference. They provide us with a sense of stability, coherence, community, and identity. Consequently they are often emotionally charged and strongly defended. Other points of view are judged against the standards set by our points of view. Viewpoints that call our frames of reference into question may be dismissed as distorting, deceptive, ill intentioned, or crazy. (p. 18)

Transformation theory emphasizes the importance of recognizing when our understandings about the world are fundamentally uprooted and challenged by experiences that do not fit with existing frames of reference. These experiences occur on a small scale when we take on different roles and responsibilities; more notably, they occur when we encounter cultural differences or develop new insights on social injustice and educational equity.

For instance, the aspiring administrator who grew up in a small town is placed in an urban school with a diverse population. She becomes aware of the class-based and racial disparities present in "achievement gaps," a pattern she had not noticed before.

When frames of reference are disrupted, need to be reframed, or even fundamentally reformed, then transformative learning takes place. The revised understanding becomes more accurate and responsive to a broadened and multifaceted perspective of reality. This idea of raising one's own and others' consciousness, of changing perspectives and shifting paradigms in this way, is fundamental to social justice leadership. Transformation theory is tied to social justice leadership in two important ways: (a) self-awareness and (b) cross-cultural understanding.

Self-Awareness

There are two aspects of self-awareness that require consideration. First is the willingness and ability to look deeply at one's own frames of reference. This requires consistent perception of one's thought patterns, underlying cognitive habits, and emotive responses.

The second aspect of self-awareness is attentiveness to the impact of our frames of reference on our understanding and decision making as well as their impact on our interpersonal and organizational interactions. This is important to social justice leadership because there are almost always aspects to one's frames of reference that are problematic from a social justice perspective. While self-awareness is a cognitive state, when manifested as humility, openness, and cognitive flexibility, it can strongly support social justice learning and leadership.

Cross-Cultural Understanding

This understanding begins by seeing one's own and others' cultural foundations as equally complex and equally valid. It is more than learning about another cultural group (e.g., stereotypes, cultural practices, and similarities and differences between and among cultural groups). It is about developing more complex familiarity of, experience with, and understanding of the "other."

From an ethical standpoint, cross-cultural understanding is similar to our earlier discussion in chapter 3 encouraging consideration of wholeness rather than division and discord. This capacity is essential to affirming the human dignity of each and every person inclusive of her or his individual and sociocultural identity.

Since one's formative frames of reference are, in part, products of one's cultural foundations, cross-cultural understanding requires transformative learning and is important for social justice leadership because of the need to work effectively with others from cultures different from our own. It is also important in discerning the presence and impact of a mono-cultural school environment and transforming it into a multicultural one.

CRITICAL THEORY

In *The Shame of the Nation*, Jonathan Kozol (2005) documented how de facto segregated education in American public schools is worsening and how African American and Hispanic students disproportionately bear the brunt of this situation. Our second theoretical lens of critical theory seeks to investigate why and how schools and systems, knowingly or unknowingly, operate in ways that systematically privilege some students while disadvantaging and marginalizing others, especially those who live in poverty and are of color, whose first language is other than English, and/or who live with disability.

For social justice leaders, critical theory is essential in understanding and addressing the processes that cause social segregation and economic stratification, as these processes result in inequalities that limit opportunities and benefits for marginalized students. Critical theory questions how such unequal practices have been sustained in school institutions and asks why these remain the status quo. This perspective is advocated by educational scholars such as Jean Anyon, Michael Apple, Lisa Delpit, Michelle Fine, Paulo Freire, Gloria Ladson-Billings, and Pedro Nogreura who challenge society's collective and dominant frames of reference that undergird and sustain inequality in and from the system.

Recognizing the larger sociopolitical context for these disparities, critical theorists such as Apple and Weis (1983) proposed the need to not only see how schooling relates to reproducing society's divisions but to consider what actions can be taken to critique, resist, and ultimately transform schooling practices. Giroux (1997) stated that individuals

> must struggle to create the conditions that enable students and others to become cultural producers who can rewrite their own experiences and perceptions by engaging with various texts, ideological positions and theories. (p. 263)

We suggest that critical theory without action is only academic, so below we present two examples of critical theory in action through equity consciousness and anti-oppressive teaching.

Equity Consciousness

This action demands looking beyond achievement test scores when locating equity concerns and considering the causes, conditions, and outcomes of educational inequities. One way to accomplish equity consciousness is to conduct equity audits, as suggested by Skrla, Scheurich, Garcia, and Nolly (2010). The audits examine what is occurring for students in different programs (e.g., gifted and talented, special education) or through different disciplinary actions evident at the classroom, school, or district level.

The process of auditing can expose more complex and nuanced patterns of how individuals are differentiated and how resources, opportunities, and punishments/rewards are distributed (Capper & Frattura, 2008; Scheurich & Skrla, 2003). For example, an audit might reveal a preponderance of African American males with special education services or an overrepresentation of middle-class, white students receiving gifted and talented services. Doing the audits can raise equity consciousness in the school organization and serve as factual narratives informing key questions of fairness and equal opportunity for all students.

Anti-Oppressive Education

Drawing from his varied teaching background (e.g., Peace Corps teacher in Nepal, middle school English teacher, summer school singing instructor), Kevin Kumashiro (2000, 2004) defined *anti-oppressive education* as a process intended to critically examine one's teaching to affirm social justice in the classroom. It acts against multiple forms of oppression, including racism, sexism, homophobia, ableism, religious oppression, classism, and any other "isms."

By targeting the processes, structures, and discourses through which privilege and oppression, normalization, and marginalization occur and perpetuate inequality, this approach aims to eliminate privilege and oppression as conditions in society. This is different from other approaches that focus on bringing equality to certain marginalized groups within the existing structure and organization of society.

Kumashiro encouraged teachers to be critical and problematize what is being taught to whom and for what ends, and how the teaching is conducted. Anti-oppressive education involves the willingness to experience the discomfort of transformative learning. It requires one "to desire change, to desire difference" (Kumashiro, 2000, p. 20), and to translate new understandings and frames of reference into different ways of being, acting, and relating.

Equity consciousness and anti-oppressive teaching are examples of how to move from critical theory to social justice action. Both offer a social justice leader concrete applications of a critical theoretical lens when applied to institutions. However, a more comprehensive theoretical grounding toward social change may be needed, and we propose organizational and social change theory to meet that requirement.

ORGANIZATIONAL AND SOCIAL CHANGE THEORIES

The third component of a social justice orientation addresses how one leads groups of people to make social justice change within organizations. Considering change at the organizational level is important because social justice change involves more than just changing the minds and actions of individuals. Instead, leading this type of change requires collective, not singular, efforts. It also involves navigating the unique structures, processes, and culture to effectively revise those structures, processes, and culture to support greater equity and social justice.

Understanding the societal nature of social justice change is important as well. Inequity and injustice are structural, functional, and societal. Leaders need to understand how inequities are held within underlying beliefs, values, and frames of reference of individuals, groups, and organizations. By knowing and understanding this, they can more effectively implement technical and structural change efforts.

Understanding the literature on organizational and social change, leaders can more readily recognize institutional and systemic inequities and commit to improve equity outcomes for a group, school, or organization. But much as critical theory has various approaches and directives, organizational and social change is informed by multiple theories from organizational development, social movements, and adult learning, all of which are directed toward different ends.

For a sampling of approaches, consider the following. Those who view schools and classrooms as sites of cultural reproduction are directed toward teaching practice and critical pedagogies. This approach emphasizes how teachers affect change in the classroom as they practice the art and craft of teaching (Giroux, 1997). Social justice school administrators might consider their role as instructional leaders in supporting this effort. Fullan (1991) reiterated that the work is not necessarily to implement innovations or instructional change but ultimately to transform the school culture through collaboration, engagement, and commitment.

At the school level, those who focus on achievement might tend to look at what critical factors relate to enhancing outcomes and narrowing the achievement gap. Ronald Edmonds's (1979) work on effective schools identified specific factors such as strong leadership, high expectations, basic skills, orderly environment, and student assessment. Bryk, Bender Sebring, Allensworth, Luppescu, and Easton (2010) updated Edmonds's work by building a framework of essential supports, recognizing the complexity of school organizations and their overlapping, intersecting subsystems.

At the macro level of district or community, advocates propose acknowledging sociocultural, political, and environmental dimensions of public education that set the context for social justice change. Rodriguez and Fabrionar (2010) posited that school leaders need to reflect upon how poverty impacts children and families in their schools in order to "align school and community resources with greater efficacy and innovation, and surface and interrupt school policies and practices that reinforce social inequality" (p. 55).

Regardless of level—classroom, school, or community—social justice leaders will likely begin by talking with their colleagues about the vision, design, and development of school reform efforts. They must be able to lead change efforts in a manner that is consistent with the end goal.

Should change be intended to create inclusive learning environments, then inclusion must be a key consideration in the change effort (Riehl, 2000). Leadership must recognize and account for the social, organizational, and transformational nature of social justice changes.

INTEGRATING THE LENSES

We intentionally tie together the three theoretical lenses toward social justice action. Beginning within the theoretical frame of *transformative learning*, self-awareness sets the stage for how one learns and alters one's own frames of reference. One can begin to question taken-for-granted assumptions and habitual responses that mask the realities of inequity and injustice and then work through the cognitive dissonance likely encountered. One can proceed toward cultural exploration to develop more complex and nuanced understandings of self and other and to foster more effective and authentic cross-cultural relationships.

Critical theory is essential because it focuses on a more comprehensive examination of the systemic nature of inequity and injustice. Leaders are directed to identify policies, patterns, and practices that might advantage some and disadvantage others, particularly along lines of class, race, gender, sexual orientation, disability, and so on. Beyond the "isms," this theoretical lens fosters a better understanding of the complex, multidimensional, and latent inequities present in public schools and school systems that must be understood when attempting to promote social justice.

Lastly, *organizational and social change theories* enable leaders to hold a broader vision for what is needed, while negotiating feasible models and strategies for making systemic, structural changes in the classroom, school, and community. Unfortunately, it is appealing to design technical and structural changes without fully examining the context and developing content knowledge that would inform right design and good outcomes. Rather than pushing forward the social justice agenda at the expense of adequate dialogue, due process, and inclusiveness, this theoretical lens encourages and supports change design and methods in which right means match justice-oriented ends.

The social justice conceptual framework we have presented is not just academic. Life experiences can be seen running through these theories, prodding us to investigate, change, and potentially transform our thinking. Here are three examples. The new dean of students, Nancy was challenged with a student body so different and diverse that none of her usual frames of reference worked sufficiently to operate in such a context. Through a heightened equity consciousness, she needed to reexamine her assumptions and reorient her priorities to better serve the students.

With a background in community organizing and a commitment to migrant workers' children, Mateo had been organizing "against the system" all his adult life. But as a school administrator, he represented that system and its teaching staff. Now his challenge was to get his teachers to think differently about the migrant workers' children they taught but not disregard their perspective and alienate them in the process.

Becoming the grandparent of a child with autism, Kofi realized he lacked sufficient knowledge of special needs for children. He sought to study how best to serve, support, and sustain his family members as well as those in his public school setting. He became more of an advocate for students with learning and other disabilities at school because of his own family's changing circumstances.

Nancy, Mateo, and Kofi all demonstrate how complicated it can be to take theory into action. In the next section, we explore impediments to realizing social justice leadership.

BARRIERS IN DOING SOCIAL JUSTICE

Among the internal barriers that leaders must address within themselves to be effective are the following: (a) deficit thinking, (b) the inability to work with difference, (c) a lack of equity consciousness, and (d) the misuse and misunderstanding of power.

Deficit Thinking

The term *deficit thinking* refers to thought patterns among educators and administrators who see students of color, students living in poverty, and other students who are marginalized as "less than" (Pollack, 2012; Walker, 2010). This is evident when educators comment that these students' parents don't value education or that those students are not capable, thus somehow not fully deserving. As a result, educators are willing to settle for less not only from these students and their families but for them as well.

Deficit thinking is detrimental to social justice because when educators have low expectations of students who are marginalized or hold negative beliefs about their families, it translates into less effective, less committed teaching and learning.

Inability to Work with Difference

Studying communication and relationships, Deborah Tannen (1999) proposed that Americans had developed an "argument culture" whereby it was culturally preferable to prove one's rightness and win an argument than to understand another viewpoint and change one's mind. Neither side understands the other, nor even cares to understand a different viewpoint.

In today's increasingly diverse society, cross-cultural encounters can often lead to numerous misunderstandings and polarization. Whether stemming from ideological, political, or cultural differences, polarization is detrimental to the well-being of a school or district. Polarization also challenges progress toward social justice because it accentuates power differences and manifests power displays in order to "get one's way." Even though polarization is so destructive, most Americans struggle with more constructive means to engage with differences. As a result, so do most school leaders.

Lack of Equity Consciousness

There is a dominant ideology that the United States is a place of fairness and justice and that inequalities and discrimination arising from the "isms" (e.g., classism, racism, sexism) are things of the past. This viewpoint denies the systemic nature of inequality and injustice, especially as it occurs disproportionately along lines of race, class, gender, ability, language, religion, and sexual orientation. Inequitable outcomes often result from systemic organizational practices and policies that are endemic to schools and found in administrator practices (Marshall & Oliva, 2010).

Many school leaders who aim to address achievement disparities may still perpetuate other forms of inequity. This is more common than one might think. When leaders are not aware of the systemic and pervasive nature of inequity and the multiple forms of oppression that occur in and through schools, they may perpetuate these tendencies of the system.

Misuse and Misunderstanding of Power

Whether formal or informal, positional or otherwise, power is a part of leadership: "[I]t circulates around the leader, is available to the leader, and must be used by the leader" (Radd, 2007, p. 185). In working for social justice, leaders often lack consciousness about their own power and the ways in which they use it. As a result, they often take missteps and misuse their power in ways that advantage some and disadvantage others. In other situations, leaders for social justice struggle to navigate the power of hierarchies and organizational structures effectively and, as a result, comply with unjust conditions or processes. Misunderstanding and misusing power can tend to perpetuate inequity and injustice rather than alleviate it.

LEADING FOR SOCIAL JUSTICE

How might a school administrator effectively use her leadership to advance social justice? Utilizing theoretical lenses and internal barriers in doing social justice work, we offer these three considerations: (a) engaging multiple perspectives and stakeholders, (b) employing an anti-oppression approach, and (c) leading for inclusion with agency and humility. These considerations provide a means for practical application of social justice principles.

Engage Multiple Perspectives and Stakeholders

It has long been demonstrated that a diverse set of perspectives and an open communication process lead to the most effective decisions with strong stakeholder support (Roberto, 2005). To obtain these diverse perspectives, one must engage a diverse set of stakeholders.

It may not be a simple task to solicit and talk with multiple stakeholders from varied backgrounds and viewpoints. Indeed, it may be easier to find those who are like-minded to gain consensus in decision making. Still, much is lost from such an approach. Although time consuming, talking with a diverse group of stakeholders who bring divergent perspectives and information to the table can mean that any decisions and plans will be well vetted. Those involved will be better informed and more likely to be supportive, thus potentially making implementation more effective.

Still, how does one go about this task? First, it requires the types of cross-cultural understanding and relationships presented earlier. The leader must be willing to engage meaningfully, intentionally, and authentically with all stakeholders. Whether those persons are different from the leader in terms of their race, ethnicity, religious or political views, or educational background, the leader's sincere effort to include and understand other perspectives will serve the organization well.

Second, the leader must be skilled at leading a diverse group through constructive exploration and resolution of the conflicts that will inevitably occur. One important strategy here is to see those conflicts, while time consuming, as necessary and valuable. If the leader can position cross-cultural and cross-group conflict in a way that engages and values varied perspectives, she or he has the opportunity to build a unified multicultural community in and for the school.

Dewey (1938) captured this idea in describing working through conflict and honoring individuals. He wrote:

> Democracy is the belief that even when needs and ends or consequences are different for each individual, the habit of amicable cooperation . . . is itself a priceless addition to life. To take as far as possible every conflict which arises—and they are bound to arise—out of the atmosphere and medium of force, of violence as a means of settlement into that of discussion and of intelligence is to treat those who disagree—even profoundly—with us as those from whom we may learn, and in so far, as friends. (p. 342)

Employ an Anti-Oppression Approach

Recall that an anti-oppression approach is targeted toward dismantling privilege and oppression wherever they occur. It does not prefer one form of oppression over another; rather it critiques the act of oppression and the systems of privilege that sustain them. An anti-oppression approach offers three distinct benefits to a social justice agenda.

First, an anti-oppression approach, by virtue of its target, is broad and inclusive. By encompassing all forms of oppression and privilege, it is possible for more stakeholders to become engaged in change efforts. For example, gay parents, staff persons living with disabilities, and community members from a religious minority may share experiences of discrimination and marginalization and thus become inspired to work together to eliminate them.

Second, the approach raises different sorts of questions than an "achievement gap" framing or a single-group focus. It addresses the systemic and pervasive nature of privilege and oppression, demanding that individuals and groups examine individual and organizational structures, policies, and culture to identify and address patterns of advantage and disadvantage. To a large degree, this allows social justice efforts to be "hard on systems" and "soft on people."

Third, the approach endorses inclusive and distributed leadership by fundamentally challenging the use of power and position to ensure these are used for liberating and democratic purposes. When leaders are willing to share power and hold their own uses of power up to scrutiny, it creates a more engaged and powerful followership. According to Dewey (1938):

> A genuinely democratic faith in peace is a faith in the possibility of conducting disputes, controversies and conflicts as cooperative undertakings in which both parties learn by giving the other a chance to express itself, instead of having one party conquer by forceful suppression of the other. (p. 342)

Lead for Inclusion with Agency and Humility

There are three important elements to this final consideration: (a) inclusion, (b) agency, and (c) humility.

First, the idea of inclusion bears additional mention and explanation here. The premise of social justice lies in expanding inclusion and rejecting the practice of exclusion. In practice, this means creating inclusive classrooms, integrated schools, multicultural staffs, and diverse decision-making bodies while rejecting tracking, segregation, unsatisfactory hiring practices, and insufficient community outreach. Beyond schools, the practice could be extending into society at large. Inclusive and integrated companies with multicultural staffs and diverse decision making that honors the experience of all employees will advance a social justice agenda.

Agency and humility go hand in hand for leaders of social justice. Agency represents a sense of confidence and efficacy that the leader must possess to combat the resilience of the system that will act to maintain the status quo. Moreover, others see the leader with positional or informal power and will have high expectations of the leadership. If the leader is not confident of her or his ability and methods to lead and effect change, attaining others' support may be difficult.

Humility is an equally important quality, fostering an inclusive and relationship-oriented approach to leadership. It is important because leaders ultimately have shortcomings in their approach, knowledge, and skills. Maintaining openness to correction, feedback, opinions, and change ensures that one will continue to improve in practice and relationships. Achieving a good balance of agency and humility is the dance of this component.

Dewey's (1938) writings on democracy stated the importance of leading for inclusion with agency and humility:

> To cooperate by giving differences a chance to show themselves because of the belief that the expression of difference is not only a right of the other person but is a means of enriching one's own life-experience, is inherent in the democratic personal way of life. (p. 342)

SUMMARY

Much as feminism and ecofeminism offer critical perspectives that inform our moral–ethical decisions, so too does the social justice leadership presented in this chapter. We defined the term and attempted to highlight some features particularly as needed in the preparation of social justice leaders. Key theoretical lenses include a theory on transformative learning evidenced through self-awareness and cross-cultural understanding, critical theory as exemplified in equity consciousness and anti-oppressive education, and organizational and social change theories needed to make reform happen.

Armed with theoretical lenses, social justice leaders will need to apply them pragmatically in daily practice. Among the challenges in doing so are internal barriers such as deficit thinking, the inability to work with difference, a lack of equity consciousness, and a misuse and misunderstanding of power.

We suggest that Dewey's understanding of democracy undergirds three components to social justice leadership: engaging multiple perspectives and stakeholders, employing an anti-oppression frame, and leading for inclusion with agency and humility. These ways emphasize the democratic leadership necessary for engaging everyone to create a truly multicultural community.

II

Methods

SIX

John Dewey and Democratic Leadership

Throughout this book, we build upon the premise that an ethic of democratic leadership—where leaders foster democratic practices in their institutions—is the most effective and desirable form of leadership available (Bryk et al., 2010; Cordeiro & Cunningham, 2013; Kramer, 2006a; Starratt, 2004). We believe this for three reasons. First, like John Dewey, we see that the problems of any group or organization occur as people associate with one another. Conflict between individuals is inevitable and, if not handled wisely, can debilitate the persons involved and even the organization that they serve. Democratic practices recognize and guide how we approach our day-to-day work by offering a framework for resolving disputes and clashes.

Second, Dewey's concept of democracy may be defined as negotiating the ethical space between the needs of the individual and the needs of the groups to which one belongs. While this means that effective leaders recognize the importance of balancing individual needs with group needs, this is not easily done.

Third, there are habitual behaviors in organizations that can restrict how we respond to complex problems. In addition, Dewey's concept of democracy accounts for the critical lenses of religious attitudes, feminism, and social justice presented in earlier chapters of this book. Democratic leaders can apply creativity and moral imagination to problems requiring new ways of doing things. In this chapter, we present the tenets of democratic leadership and illustrate how democratic leadership might be enacted in the following case.

NANCY'S DILEMMA

Nancy is an administrator at Garden Middle School in a large, suburban school district. While the suburb has been traditionally white, as the result of an NAACP lawsuit the district reluctantly joined a voluntary desegregation consortium with twelve other school districts. As a consequence, they began receiving a small but significant number of students of color who were bused in from the nearby metropolitan center. This has been a very different experience for the fairly homogeneous, upper middle-class school district. The result of the busing has meant heightened racial–ethnic tensions among the students, antagonism among some of the faculty, hostility from parents, and a tough ethical situation for Nancy.

Serving as dean of students, Nancy is responsible for all student concerns, from monitoring attendance to administering disciplinary actions. She deals directly with the upsets caused by student misconduct in classrooms, halls, and lunchroom, as adolescents often act out their frustrations. Nancy has also been deeply committed to ensuring educational equity and promoting equal opportunity. A white person, she has done volunteer work with minority communities in the urban center and has learned about the hardships that families in poverty face. In addition, her graduate studies in leadership and critical theories have helped her become more aware of the racial–ethnic tension in her community and school.

Transported daily by bus into the Garden district, these students of color are struggling to adapt to their new school environment. There is little integration between the whites and students of color. The new students usually cluster together during recess and at lunch. Some have taken on a "don't mess with me" attitude that has led to fights among the students. But teachers seem to see only the students of color at fault. Once while Nancy was walking the hall, two eighth-grade boys, one black and one white, came bounding up to her. "Are you coming to the basketball game tonight?" they asked breathlessly. Before she could respond, a classroom teacher came out of his room and dressed down the black student but not the white student for wearing saggy pants. The teacher said nothing to him despite his saggy pants.

When Nancy raised these concerns with the faculty, teachers accused her of taking the side of the new students even if that was not the case. Many of these teachers have more years of seniority than she has at Garden Middle School, and they can make life difficult for anyone with a different point of view. Having spent years teaching a traditional secondary school curriculum, many teachers retain habits that have worked in the past but are now being challenged to teach differently with little training and support for differentiated instruction. Some teachers are already grumbling about how these "new kids" will bring the school's test scores down.

Nancy is in a similar bind with the parents. The voluntary desegregation plan allows parents outside the district to choose to send their kids to Garden Middle School. Understandably, it is a difficult choice to send one's children to another school district across town, requiring long bus rides each day. In making that choice, parents sought assurances from the school that their children would receive the same or better-quality education than at their neighborhood schools.

Now parents are frustrated by the school's lack of sensitivity to their children's needs. The administration and teachers seem to have little experience with minority students and are hardly welcoming. Almost all of the communication from the school to the parents raises their anxiety level even further. When Nancy contacted the parents, some asked blunt questions and made emotional demands on behalf of their children.

In one case, when a new student got into a fight, the parent demanded that the school *not* implement the standard procedure of a three-day suspension. Nancy felt she had no choice in the matter, and the parent called her a "racist white cracker." Despite feeling hurt over the remark, she could understand the parent's concerns. If kids were suspended so easily and school was not where they wanted to be in the first place, then the punishment achieved the wrong outcome. It might also place an economic burden on a family already having difficulty making ends meet.

The school principal is too busy to deal with these matters directly. He has been frequently off campus at district meetings, leaving Nancy to handle complaints and frustrations on her own. His major concern has centered on No Child Left Behind and retaining his school's record of sterling academic achievement. There is a chance that Garden Middle might fall below par, and that would get his attention right away.

Nancy is in a very uncomfortable ethical position. As dean of students, she needs to deal fairly and consistently with all Garden Middle students. It is part of her obligation as an administrator. For some faculty, her job is enforcing strong rules that are applied in the same way for every student regardless of circumstance. She feels obligated to care especially for these new students, ensuring that they make a good transition to Garden Middle. It might entail providing interventions that are more appropriate and equitable for them even though they are in the minority. This action would be aligned with her deep personal commitment to equity and social justice.

CONDITIONS CALLING FOR DEMOCRATIC LEADERSHIP

If we apply Dewey's theoretical construct of democracy to Nancy's situation, at least three conditions call for democratic leadership. First, Dewey would have us consider problems of association that create conflicts through social order distinctions, changes from old to new, and private–public interest differences. Second, he would ask about balancing the needs of individuals with the groups to which they belong. Third, Dewey would propose that we explore and deconstruct habitual behaviors among the school members to resolve Nancy's ethical situation. Each condition suggests possible actions toward resolution.

Problems of Association

Dewey saw conflict as an inevitable part of human interaction, as human beings make demands upon each other. And these demands are sometimes at odds with an individual's desires. Calling these conflicts "problems of association," Dewey categorized them as (a) social order conflicts ("class and mass") whereby a dominant group, be it social, political, or economic, seeks to maintain its hegemonic position with a subordinate group/s; (b) change conflicts ("traditional versus alternative") whereby the old wishes to preserve its forms over a newer or different alternative; and (c) private versus public conflicts whereby private interests clash with public ones (Dewey & Tufts, 1932a, pp. 325–327).

Social Order Conflicts

In terms of hierarchy in school organizations, classroom teachers generally report to their administrator. The principal is often solely responsible for hiring, supervising, and evaluating the teachers and staff in the school. In turn, principals are usually hired and evaluated by their superior. This could be the superintendent of the district or a designee such as the deputy in charge of schools. A superintendent might be hired and appointed by a school board.

The organizational hierarchy is clearly delineated between teacher and principal, between principal and superintendent, and between superintendent and school board (Cordeiro & Cunningham, 2013). Often, what is not so clear is how parents and community and business leaders figure into the social order. In some schools and districts, these groups may exert considerable influence upon what policies are enacted and how schools are supported. In other cases, they may have very little influence in what happens at school or simply may act to reinforce the administrators' wishes.

As dean of students, Nancy is specifically responsible for monitoring the academic and social welfare of each student at Garden Middle. In providing support services, she is at the same hierarchical level as the classroom teachers since she does not directly supervise them and has no authority over them. Yet she must work with them on matters of discipline and student conduct, often communicating their concerns to the parents. She serves as a go-between for the parents and the school. Ultimately she must answer to the principal, as he has the final say on student behavioral expectations. She is also subject to his review and appraisal of her performance of duties and responsibilities.

To examine potential social order conflicts, we note that Garden Middle School is situated within a school district in the state. The principal reports to the district superintendent and, therefore, must deal with district matters that have taken him away from the school. Further, he must attend to federal and state mandates, ensuring that his school meets the standards and achievement benchmarks required by statute. His performance as school principal will be assessed based upon whether he is successful in doing so. Using the category of social order conflicts, we can examine the school within a complex bureaucracy and question how its leadership must respond to all stakeholders as well as to federal and state expectations for success.

Change Conflicts

This problem of association occurs between the old and the new. One group seeks to preserve what has been before and might hold that school traditions are at stake if change is enacted. The other seeks to do things differently, possibly in better and more progressive ways. However, those newer ways have not been tested, and the group advocating change struggles to assert its influence on the organization. As Machiavelli wrote in *The Prince*, "Nothing is more dangerous or difficult than introducing a new order of things" (quoted in Badaracco, 2006, p. 76).

Dewey recognized that old-versus-new conflicts take on a larger meaning than that of conserving the past versus adopting alternatives for the future. The past is seen as socially organized in that it is a known way that has led to stability for the group. The future is nebulous because new proposals have little or no credibility and are untested in the organization. Further, those promoting newer forms may have little power or resources under the current system. They may be more critical of the existing organizational structure since their experience of organizations is one of lacking resources.

Garden Middle School is operating under its old habits and routines. Students who have attended the school have been mostly white and affluent, coming directly from the suburban community. They have grown up with Garden's way of doing things. According to some of the faculty and staff, the existing rules and routines have worked in the past and should work now. Some teachers are concerned that if they change their approach, they will water down their curricular standards.

Unfortunately things are not working for the newcomers. The new students bring different academic and social backgrounds along with different needs, desires, and expectations. This does not mean that school rules don't apply; it does mean that there will be a conflict between old and new cultures. In this case, there are racial–ethnic, as well as class, differences to add to the forced merger. Teachers have not had to deal with these kinds of differences; neither have they been given training or support in delivering differentiated instruction to serve the newer students. They may resort to habitual ways of doing things that will not work with the new challenges and different needs that the students bring.

Nancy is concerned that if a change is not made in the way that the school approaches the new students, then they will be lost or, worse, will act out their frustration in destructive ways. However, her concerns have little credibility with many of the senior faculty because the students represent an unknown future that is of questionable value. As well, Nancy has made limited inroads with the parents because, as school personnel, she is viewed distrustfully. Thus, the ethical conflict of conserving old forms versus introducing newer ways is evident in Nancy's situation.

Private–Public Conflicts

This problem of association is present whenever private interests and public agency clash. Nancy has "private interests" in that she wants these new students to succeed. Individual students and their parents also have "private interests" to ensure their needs are met. As a public agency, the school has shared or mutually agreed upon ways of resolving conflict, which are present in the rules, regulations, and policies that are in place. These may or may not be appropriate to the situation at hand.

Nancy desires that the discipline rules in this case be individually adjusted to meet what she perceives to be the specific needs of the students involved. However, in the interest of fair and equal treatment, Garden Middle School faculty members want school rules to be upheld in a consistent manner. By doing so, they are upholding the public agency of their school. At the same time, the faculty and staff probably do not want the school to be thought of as uncaring or even racist. This negative image could become a mechanism for leverage by Nancy and the parents as they negotiate this conflict.

Balancing Individual and Group Needs

The second condition calling for democratic leadership is that the needs of individuals and the needs of groups often conflict. While this condition has been discussed in problems of association, there is a more specific way to point to problems that arise between individuals and groups. To paraphrase Dewey, leadership dilemmas are not so much between individuals but between groups of individuals disagreeing over some larger idea or social order.

Such conflicts can be personalized at the individual level. When things do not go our way, we tend to seek out a cause that is much more personal or individualized: "He doesn't like me" or "That teacher always picks on me." However, rarely does just one person feel the fallout from any given conflict. So what appears to be a conflict between individuals probably relates to the group.

As the students of color became frustrated with Garden Middle School teachers, they began to act out by fighting with the white students. These individual acts clearly had racial overtones. In one case, Nancy implemented a three-day suspension on a black student for fighting. The parent responded by calling her a racist and viewing the actions of the school as a racist institution. Nancy began to fear that the parents would create a public spectacle that could negatively affect the entire school community.

In a similar way, the teachers enlarged the incident by viewing it as a threat to the academic integrity of Garden Middle. The combination of the academic integrity issue and the racial tensions dramatically changed the situation. What had been students who manifested their own internal conflicts by fighting became a conflict between a group of school personnel defending its high academic standards and a group of irate parents objecting to its racism.

John Dewey felt that the greatest challenge of democracy was balancing the individual needs of the members with the overall needs of the communal group. He proposed a test for whether the needs of the individual or the group were out of balance. Dewey believed that the role of any group was to support what we would call its members' self-actualization (Maslow, 1987) and what Dewey reffered to as "growth" (Noddings, 1995). At the same time, growth of any individual should not get in the way of the group's ability to support its members' individual growth.

The test, while simple, is actually quite complicated. How are individual needs to be determined? To what extent does one individual represent the group as a whole? How are roles defined for individuals and groups? How does the leader monitor what is occurring? Who determines whether a threshold is reached that tips the equation toward one side or the other?

What are some of individual and group needs present in Nancy's situation? The students of color need to find success and acceptance in their new school—a place that appears to be hostile to them. Their parents need to feel that the school is treating their children fairly while providing a quality educational environment for them. The faculty and staff believe that their professional integrity is tied to enforcing rules and regulations consistently. Many also believe that their academic standards are being challenged and they need to be able to respond effectively to meet all students' needs. Garden Middle School as a whole will need to operate in an orderly and safe manner. Hopefully they will seek to provide a caring school environment as well as a rigorous academic one.

Nancy needs to feel that she is advancing equitable treatment and improving the lot of all the students. She must consider all at Garden Middle, not only the newest students. She also needs to be supported by the school administrator responsible for the school. While balancing these needs will not be easy, recognizing what is demanded and what is at stake marks the start of working Nancy's dilemma.

Habitual Responses

The third condition of social interaction that calls for democratic leadership relates to the habitual responses on the part of members as well as the organization. Identifying this condition may seem unnecessary in light of the discussion about change conflicts referenced in the problems of association. However, with change conflicts, the parties on either side are consciously seeking either to conserve the old ways or to redefine ways to respond. Both sides are aware of what they are advocating and why they want either constancy or change. In the case of habitual responses, members may not be aware of their behaviors or actions.

Habits and routines are everyday behaviors that form our ways of doing things, frequently taken for granted and often unconsciously executed (Conley & Enomoto, 2009). In school organizations, habitual activities can include how class attendance is taken, how courses are scheduled each year, or how personnel are routinely evaluated.

Dewey suggested that habitual responses serve us well in that we do not have to think about performing these behaviors, thus freeing us to attend to other matters. But habits can also stifle members' behavior, curb innovation, and structure decision making when problems occur. They may persist when no longer necessary or appropriate because particular external pressures exist or internal constraints limit changes (Feldman, 2000). Individuals and groups might also resist making any changes. Routines in organizations may even restrict our ways of defining problems and seeking solutions.

In the Garden Middle School case, Nancy recognizes the inadequacy of the school's habitual responses to the students coming in from the metropolitan center. Seeking to do business as usual, many faculty members appear to be unaware of the challenges of the new situation. Their successes in the past might blind them as to how to deal with students who bring different needs to Garden Middle. Likewise, the parents might be operating out of habitual responses to institutional and societal racism. For both groups, parents and teachers, the responses could be unconsciously executed.

For Nancy, negotiating the space between the school and parents is complicated for several reasons. First, she is a well-educated white woman who is aware of the privilege brought by her class and race. She believes that most of her colleagues at Garden Middle do not recognize their own privilege, either socioeconomic or otherwise.

Another reason is that Nancy can identify aspects of racism at Garden Middle School based on her six years there. She also might contribute to it even if she believes that racism is wrong and fights to overcome it. To the parents, she does represent the school and may be viewed negatively because of it.

A third reason is that Nancy is aware that Garden Middle School has operated successfully for over twenty-five years in terms of academic achievement. She is confronting a long-standing habitual way of doing things ("the Garden Middle School way") that has been appropriate and successful in the past. Perhaps individual student conflicts and external pressures from parents and community have not pushed Garden Middle beyond its habitual responses.

DEMOCRACY AND DEMOCRATIC LEADERSHIP

We have been using the term *democracy* throughout this chapter specifically and throughout the book generally. Now it is time to show how democratic leadership addresses the conflicts related to problems of association mentioned above and faced constantly in a pluralistic school organization.

In writing about democracy, Dewey did not necessarily mean a government structure (e.g., three separate branches of government) or political form (e.g., free elections, voter representation). Rather, the term was more about living in association with others. "A democracy is more than a form of government; it is primarily a mode of associated living, of conjoint communicated experience" (Dewey, 1916, p. 87). An overarching meta-ethic, democracy guides how we ought to approach living with each other. Dewey saw the true measure of democracy as the discursive, dialogical quality between individuals and groups and their mutual growth, which makes democracy viable and necessary.

Recall in Chapter 2, democracy is seen as a way of negotiating the potential growth of the individual with the needs of the group and vice versa. Negotiation can lead to individual development as well as to achievement of the group's purpose. To do this, individuals must take a responsible share in providing the direction for the group's activities. Dewey (1916) stated:

> From the standpoints of the groups, [democracy] demands liberation of the potentialities of members of a group in harmony with the interests and goods which are common. Since every individual is a member of many groups, this specification cannot be fulfilled except when differ-

ent groups interact flexibly and fully in connection with other groups. (p. 147)

Dewey saw the need for conscious sharing among members and the free association among differing groups. He believed that this kind of exchange would promote individual as well as group development and progress.

Recognizing that individuals were members of many social groups and that communication was essential to fulfilling individual potential, Dewey believed that the communicated experience was key to achieving democratic ends. What did he mean by "communicated experience"? The following is illustrative:

> Try the experiment of communicating, with fullness and accuracy, some experience to another, especially if it be somewhat complicated, and you will find your own attitude toward your experience changing; otherwise you resort to expletives and ejaculations. The experience has to be formulated in order to be communicated. To formulate requires getting outside of it, seeing it as another would see it, considering what points of contact it has with the life of another so that it may be got into such form that he can appreciate its meaning. (Dewey, 1916, pp. 9–10)

In the social endeavor of communicating with others, Dewey identified processes of reconsideration, revision, meaning making, and ultimately education. "When communication occurs, all natural events are the subject of reconsideration and revision; they are re-adapted to meet the requirements of conversation, whether it be public discourse or that preliminary discourse termed thinking" (Dewey, 1938, p. 166).

Accordingly, the link between communication and democracy cannot be overstated. Democracy "demand[s] *communication* [italics in original] as a prerequisite" (Dewey, 1927, p. 152), for "[s]ociety not only continues to exist *by* transmission, *by* communication, but it may fairly be said to exist *in* transmission, *in* communication [italics in original]" (Dewey, 1916, p. 4). By communicating with one another, we create our societies. We construct the social groups, their meanings and identities, through our words, symbols, and actions. We specify our membership and define who we are in association with our group affiliations. Only if the communication is open, shared, and grounded in truth seeking, can we begin to form social structures that can handle the diverse needs of our society. Dewey believed that democracy required this kind of communication to thrive.

Dewey advocated that we communicate in a way that makes each one of us refer our actions to the beliefs, needs, and actions of others. In other words, we must "get outside our own experience" and relate to the others' perspectives and experiences. For example, if Nancy approaches her dilemma from a democratic ethic, she must begin to understand the diverse perspectives presented by the students, parents, teachers, and principal.

Listening to all the different groups is a start. It seems a logical first step but will not be easy because Nancy has already taken action and might not appear to be open to some teachers or parents. Getting outside her own experience might mean suspending her judgments and refraining from voicing an opinion. The emphasis will be on understanding the other person's needs and desires in this situation. By listening to his or her heartfelt concerns, she will be able to see more comprehensively what is needed for the school.

Nancy will also need to communicate between groups and get people to listen to each other. For now, the lines are so clearly delineated that there can be only winners and losers. How can she address this challenge when clearly she is in a very difficult and tenuous position? For this, Dewey would suggest the use of moral imagination.

MORAL IMAGINATION

Nancy's situation calls into question which group is right. Is it the parents or the teachers? Taking the approach that one side is right and the other is wrong, Nancy will most certainly fail to serve either group. She needs to understand the parents' concerns as well as gain their trust in working for their children's best interests. She also needs to encourage the teachers to work with her, connecting with those who might be supportive as well as listening carefully to those who might be opposing her perspective. If teachers need more support and professional development, how could she provide that?

If Nancy sees the parents' and teachers' concerns as mutually exclusive, then she will not be able to influence the sides toward a positive outcome. She will need to find the common ground that can unite them while doing some creative problem solving to respond to the situation at hand. In addition to excellent communication skills, she will need to employ a more creative set of skills and be morally imaginative.

Stephen Fesmire (2003), a scholar of John Dewey's philosophy, identified two main themes in Dewey's moral imagination. The first theme is "empathetic projection," whereby one imagines the other person's "aspirations, interests, and worries as our own" (p. 65). Dewey began with empathy in order to discern what it would be like to be the other rather than superimpose one's views upon others.

The other theme relates to moral imagination being a tool or skill set for yielding good ends. This might involve the skill of asking pertinent yet challenging questions or facilitating discussions with individuals or groups to determine what is most desired. It could also be about rehearsing consequences that might be likely given certain actions or strategies.

In summarizing the two themes, Fesmire stated that "[i]magination in Dewey's central sense is the capacity to concretely perceive what is before us in light of what could be" (p. 65).

Demonstrating moral imagination as a leader involves steering the process toward uncertain ends, negotiating the space between different and often clashing groups, and demonstrating bold action and moral courage. It requires patience, commitment, and determination to engage in the process.

Dewey noted that imaginative persons are often condemned for their ideas. Only later might their ideas be acknowledged and possibly recognized as beneficial. Because of this, exercising moral imagination may feel futile or fanciful. However, if we are to truly negotiate the vast range of different needs and perceptions in our society, we must be morally imaginative and promote the kind of creative thinking necessary. In essence, moral imagination can ensure that the requirements of democratic ethics are met.

RELIGIOUS ATTITUDES, FEMINISM, SOCIAL JUSTICE

At this point, the reader might be asking, "How is the philosophy of John Dewey, a white male pragmatist of the early twentieth century, relevant to the diverse leadership needs today?" We propose that Dewey's time and ours show remarkable parallels. While Dewey was concerned about the great waves of new immigrants from Europe assimilating into the American society of his time, we find similar ethical tensions in accommodating the immigrants, undocumented aliens, and war refugees in our time. Like us, Dewey was very concerned with issues of social justice, such as inequities because of poverty, race–ethnicity, gender, and disability.

Not a religious man, Dewey spoke of the societal need for a "common faith" (cited in a book by that title published in 1934). He believed that the society that supports the individual growth of the person and the free exchange of ideas between groups while holding itself accountable to the betterment of all its members needed a quasi-civil religion. He wrote of this need in religious terms citing actions that we might characterize as liturgical in reinforcing the common society necessary for human growth and development.

Nancy's case illustrates what could happen when the fabric of civil faith is torn and neither party feels any satisfaction toward resolution of its conflict. For a society to work in a way that results in the growth of its members, privilege must be acknowledged yet downplayed; resolution to conflict must accommodate the needs of all concerned. Dewey saw democracy as that civil religion providing an overarching meta-ethic by which resolution of inevitable conflicts could be judged.

Another example might be seen in the work of Charlotte Haddock Siegfried, a modern feminist pragmatist. She saw Dewey's advocacy for suffrage, along with his willingness to partner with women such as Ella Flagg Young, superintendent of Chicago schools, and Jane Addams, founder of Hull House, as indicative of his commitment to a pragmatic feminist perspective (Maher, 2001). To his credit, Dewey was a charter member of the NAACP, advocating for the equal rights of persons of color. His philosophy and values did not allow any one group to become overly privileged, seeing privilege as an impediment to democracy.

As a caution, we acknowledge that Dewey's times were not our times. Critics such as Lagemann (1996) commented that he wrote about the role of women in the family in "confused and muddled" ways. Despite recognizing the rapidly changing role of women in the early twentieth century, he was still a product of his times and did not exercise the moral imagination that he so passionately advocated throughout his career.

So to answer the question of where religious attitudes, feminism, and social justice might fit in a schema inspired by Dewey's philosophy, it is probably safe to assume that these considerations would be well within his thinking but that his own life experiences restricted his frames of reference. In this particular case it is easy to see religious attitudes, feminism, and social justice implications, as they complement Dewey's understanding of modern circumstances.

In terms of feminism, Garden Middle School has a male principal, yet the frontline protagonists for most conflicts at the school are women—the women teachers, mothers of the students of color, and the female dean of students. Nancy's situation is not unique. It could be argued that she is trying to fit her feminist experience into an institution designed by and for men. But for Nancy it is important that her understanding be translated into pragmatic action. John Dewey would understand this.

ETHICAL TENSIONS IN THE CASE

Facing an ethical dilemma, Nancy recognizes that she is responsible for upholding the policies and procedures of the district—whether they are products of privilege or not. This is why the "racist" accusation stung her so hard. She feels like a racist in this situation. Privately, she wonders why she cannot address the issues underlying the conflicts taking place and why it is not possible to effect the rules in a way that is more cognizant of the needs of the new students and their families. She sees the faculty group taking precedence through habit over the individuals in this situation. On the other hand, teachers see any attempt to treat the children differently as being ultimately harmful. Both parents and teachers see Nancy as part of the problem because she seeks to uphold the old order as well as to question it.

Yet Nancy has numerous tools that can be imaginatively utilized. At her disposal is the ability to bring people together. She can lead all the participants through creative processes that imagine different strategies for addressing the situation and their possible outcomes. She can encourage empathy and demonstrate active listening. Or Nancy might rely on the habits of old. So far, habits have gotten her into a conflict, where winners take all and losers may literally be left behind. Democratic ethics demand that she question habitual responses and encourage the imaginative. Dewey (1916) observed,

> The extension in space of the number of individuals who participate in an interest so that each has to refer his own action to that of others, and to consider the action of others to give point and direction to his own, is equivalent of the breaking down of those barriers of class, race, and national territory which kept men from perceiving the full import of their activity. (p. 87)

In other words, Dewey saw the import of morally imaginative action toward the goal of a more equitable social order. In addition, the religious attitudinal, feminist, and social justice lenses can offer direction and guidance to Nancy in this situation.

SUMMARY

In this chapter, Dewey's ethic of democratic leadership was proposed as an effective means to engage with others and strive toward collaboration. Key to developing democratic leadership is identifying three conditions calling for democracy and employing appropriate tools to facilitate it. Dewey proposed that we identify problems of association (i.e., conflicts due to social order, change, and private/public interests), balance individuals and group needs, and become aware of habitual responses to problems. Nancy's ethical dilemma at Garden Middle School is used as a case for considering these three conditions.

Throughout the chapter, we viewed democracy to be an overarching meta-ethic that guides us in how to approach the ethical dilemmas occurring in association with each other. It promotes negotiating for the potential growth of individuals within the context of their groups. It values communicating openly and freely to understand the needs and concerns of all. It advises exercising moral imagination, boldness, and courage to address the complex issues of multifaceted social groups. In the next chapter we will explore more completely an inquiry method for this kind of democratic leadership.

SEVEN

An Inquiry Method for Working Ethical Problems

In this chapter, we present an inquiry method for negotiating and working through ethical situations in various settings. The method was developed through our observation of and practical experiences with leaders from all manner of institutions. Over the past decade, it has become a linchpin for a doctoral ethics course in which students examine their values and beliefs, analyze their leadership challenges from an ethical standpoint, and apply principles toward resolutions. Working the method has led our students to experiencing personal and professional growth through resolving the challenges that they face.

The method is directly informed by John Dewey's notions of democracy and democratic practices. As defined in chapter 6, democracy is a meta-ethic to respond to the diverse needs of individuals and groups, particularly as they come into conflict with one another. Leaders need to be able to investigate problems with openness and honesty, communicating freely with all parties involved. They need to know how to systematically reflect upon intended actions and likely consequences for the constituencies whom they serve. Ultimately their work involves caring for everyone their institution touches.

We also draw from Stephen Fesmire's (2003) application of moral imagination in working creatively toward meaningful and relevant solutions. While imagination and creativity might lead to sometimes painful conclusions, Fesmire contended that it is far better to face situations honestly than to pretend otherwise.

> What is most at stake in moral life is not some quantifiable pleasure or pain, but "what kind of person one is to become" and what kind of world is to develop. These questions are explored in imagination. (p. 76)

Dewey's democratic practices and Fesmire's moral imagination provide the foundation for our inquiry method. To describe it more fully, we first clarify the nature of an ethical problem for which the method was designed, as this determines whether one would commit the resources necessary to make such an inquiry. We also consider how to define the method's usefulness. We propose that a suitable method for ethical deliberation needs two critical components, namely, discernment and action for leaders to negotiate skillfully toward resolution. These components are found in the four phases of this inquiry method, and we illustrate the phases in a case of a struggling organization.

DEFINING ETHICAL PROBLEMS

It is important to clarify what we mean by an ethical problem or predicament. For some people, this refers to a conundrum with multiple options that have equal value. For example, in trying to make a new employee hire, we may need to choose between two equally qualified candidates. If there are two similar choices, then no matter who is hired, the institution will gain a good employee.

But suppose that the choice is between two very different applicants, where selecting one over the other might negatively affect one program or another. Depending on the selected hire, a program or perhaps a department might gain or lose based on the hiring decision. No matter what decision is made, it feels like a lose–lose for both sides. This would make for an ethical dilemma in which neither choice is optimal.

Most difficult ethical problems are extremely complex, particularly if multiple persons are involved in the deliberation. This can complicate how decisions are made and what consequences result. As the leader of an organization, your decision may not be about the right course. Rather, you must assist people representing multiple perspectives to come to some form of agreement whereby no one is absolutely thrilled with the options available. Some leaders choose to resolve this by deciding themselves. This could minimize some deliberative angst if the problem is sufficiently contentious, but it may create other negative consequences such as feeling that the leader does not listen or stifles other points of view.

In addition, the situation might have a unique context and cast of characters. For example, in selecting an employee, the leader might have a workable approach to resolve the hiring. Thus it is less of a dilemma (a problem with multiple choices of equal but differing value) than it is a tough decision (one that is unpleasant but necessary to make) as part of one's job (Kidder, 1995).

A novice administrator might not have thought through the implications of the selection and hiring in terms of responses by others in the organization. That would be students, faculty, staff, parents, and others. There might be consequences related to those outside and possibly in the community at large. Then, the problem may seem to be more complex, even quite messy and muddled.

In sum, a truly difficult ethical problem involves a complexity of individual and group choices related to values of right and wrong to be deliberated and resolved. What might be a small problem for one leader may be more challenging for someone else. Individuals or groups may also be polarized over issues in the particular situation. Or there might be larger social, economic, or political issues that create more tensions in resolving the problem. The relative experience of the leadership, the multiple perspectives of the stakeholders, and the involvement of each participating decision maker can affect working ethical problems. These factors force us to probe more deeply into the situation.

DEFINING AN INQUIRY METHOD

How does a leader step beyond reflecting about values and beliefs to recognizing diverse perspectives? How might she or he take concerted action toward resolving the situation and actually lead others? We believe that the answers actually lie in these questions. Leaders need some approach of inquiry that is both reflective and active, that acknowledges the complexity of ethical dilemmas while fitting within the kind of work that leaders need to do to be effective.

Numerous ethical methods exist but we have found some to be so complicated that we are not inclined to use them. Alternatively, there are methods that constrain creativity and progressive thinking. Those too are inadequate for problem solving and decision making. We believe there is a need for a straightforward yet dynamic way to sort through these ethical dilemmas.

To be useful, a method for ethical inquiry must meet four criteria. First, we believe that the method needs to be exploratory, taking into account as much as can be known about the given situation. Anything and everything might be viewed as data—multiple perspectives, people's feelings, historical precedents, cultural rituals and routines, rules, regulations, and resources. In short, everything that relates to the problem needs to be considered. It should also include exploring meaning. Why is this situation important? What does it mean to the individuals involved? A useful inquiry method must enable a leader to candidly describe the problem as it truly is, not as it is desired to be.

Second, no dilemma or problem remains static over time. New information arises, old information becomes less credible, different perspectives become available, and people's views evolve. We believe that the method must be able to accommodate these changes, reflecting the dynamic nature of the process. This also means that the method is iterative. Faced with complex dilemmas, we might work toward a partial resolution but keep returning again and again as other factors play out.

Third, we see moral imagination as integral to the method, beginning with identifying the problem through resolving it. We emphasize that moral imagination is not moral permissiveness; these are two very different phenomena. Moral imagination and creativity foster a spectrum of possibilities to consider along with cultural and other standards that might determine choices made.

Moral permissiveness, by contrast, infers "anything goes," especially when the consequences are desirable to one or more constituencies. There is little regard for the contextual variables that might determine whether a course of action is eventually successful. As noted in chapter 2 on ethical tensions, identifying duties and virtues to which leaders and followers feel loyalty is critical to moral imagination but not necessarily in a morally permissive environment. This recognition balances the consequentialism to which leaders must give their attention.

Fourth, we believe that an inquiry method should result in the strengthening of participants' capacity for moral action as well as the group's capacity for growth. If personal and professional growth is not expected as a result of an inquiry approach to these challenging ethical predicaments, then the method is very limited in scope and use. What good is it to continue to rehash the same problems of practice if we do not get better as we work them? If we are to become more effective in working with people, then we need to develop our capacity as democratic leaders, promoting the well-being of others. This goes for individuals, groups, and whole organizations.

DISCERNMENT AND ACTION

Based upon inquiry, the method that we propose moves synergistically back and forth from processes of discernment and analysis to imaginative action. It is an act that pragmatists describe as "experimental" because both antecedents and consequential factors need to be considered. Antecedents such as one's personal background and professional experiences help to contextualize the problem, while reviewing consequences helps us rehearse the various possible effects of any action even before they occur. Discernment and action make for a dynamic, iterative method of inquiry.

For our purposes, the term *discernment* means engaging in reflection to bring about individual or group understanding and clarity. Sometimes gaining clarity may be incremental, as the facts of a case may emerge in piecemeal fashion. It may also involve moments of insight or inspiration, those "ahas" that come after much deliberation and reflection to make sense out of the situation. In either case, discernment may be thought of as more of an internal process whereas action is more overt and external.

When we speak of action, we mean behaviors that can be observed by others. Whereas discernment happens as participants engage in thinking through their own perceptions, action occurs when those perceptions are shared or when the whole group becomes more cognizant of a strategy to be taken. Action involves doing something to move the problem forward, be it seeking input from others or communicating about issues or concerns.

The following case illustrates how discernment and action can work in tandem.

SPCO DILEMMA

Over the years the St. Paul Chamber Orchestra (SPCO), a well-known and highly respected professional ensemble of thirty musicians, had managed to make its financial obligations, sometimes profitably and sometimes just barely. Within the past eight years the SPCO has resolved its financial obligations in two diametrically opposed ways. In presenting the DIRR inquiry method, we present these two approaches.

In 2005, the SPCO had enjoyed a remarkable run of well-known conductors and an international reputation of musical excellence. However, after the departure of their longtime music director Hugh Wolfe, the SPCO was faced with the problem of finding a new director along with the financial expenses of running such a search. The governing board of the SPCO needed to decide whether to hire a "big name" director to attract season ticket holders, realizing that such a choice might be too expensive for the orchestra. Alternatively, they could hire a relatively unknown conductor for the position and stay within their budget.

For two years, the board struggled with this decision—either hire a well-known music director or build a reputation for an up-and-coming maestro. As defined, the problem led them to one conclusion—that the SPCO needed a music director to lead the ensemble. And why not? They had always had a music director! With this determined and finances considered, the board decided to hire a relatively unknown conductor from an even smaller ensemble in Milwaukee. Unfortunately, the individual did not generate the kind of excitement that the board had hoped. Failing to attract the public's interest with the new music director, the SPCO's financial situation continued to worsen. By the end of the first year of the director's contract, there was a huge operating budget deficit.

This narrative exemplifies Dewey's observation that people do not usually accept facts that contradict their previously held views. He noted that we construct a habitual reality that might have served us well up to the present situation. The SPCO board members could see the solution only in terms of affording to hire a new music director. That habitual response restricted their possibilities and pushed them into a situation that was financially worse. Only then were they forced to consider alternatives and initiate a different response.

We would argue that to arrive at an ethical solution, leaders must be willing to examine and critique their own views with as much scrutiny as they give to others. Critical to such an examination is the leader's attitude, being open and willing to model sharing and self-scrutiny while asking the same of all other participants. This attitude promotes the necessary investigation and analysis of the problem. It takes a situation beyond protecting one's perceptions to describing most accurately the reality from many points of view.

Such reflection also raises questions that most leaders face in tough situations. What information should be shared with everyone? Is there a need to restrict some information? Might there be potential damage to others or negative consequences resulting from sharing everything? Leadership needs to reflect on when and how to share information to promote openness while not causing harm.

In getting back to the SPCO case, the board did decide to share the financial situation. Once the musicians became aware of the grave circumstances, they immediately perceived the possibility of laying off full-time members and having part-timers play a larger role with the group. Most musicians agreed that this would have been a disaster for the SPCO. Chamber orchestras are finely tuned ensembles in which the members get to know each other's artistic musicianship so well that they can predict musical responses from their fellow musicians, resulting in an integrated sound. They develop a unified sense of what to do in any piece of music, and this results in tight, clean performance that is much more difficult to attain with a full-sized symphony orchestra.

Knowing this, the board members made the unprecedented move to open their books to the musicians in an effort to find alternatives to the destruction of the orchestra as they had known it. This was a remarkable occurrence. Suppose that, embarrassed at not resolving the SPCO's financial problems, the board members had kept the operating deficit a secret from the musicians until the problem could no longer be hidden. The long-term effects on the orchestra would have been devastating. At the time, the board members recognized that with information shared, the musicians could freely discuss it and be involved in its resolution.

In our inquiry method, discernment shifts toward taking action. This occurs in each of the method's four phases so that timing can be discerned in an ongoing manner. Once there is knowledge of desired outcomes, then actions can be plotted and carried out. Our experience is that specific action toward problem solving is usually embedded within the dilemma itself and, thus, informed by the continual process of discernment.

The SPCO musicians chose to hold their professional group together by taking a 20 percent pay cut to meet the orchestra's financial obligations. We suspect that embedded in the SPCO was the culture of a chamber group—a small, intimate ensemble of specifically trained musicians. Such groups are not made up of interchangeable parts. Over the long-term the players had developed expertise and camaraderie, bonding them together. For the SPCO, the act of taking a pay cut, while not desirable, was preferable to breaking up the ensemble.

Appropriate actions become clearer as information is shared, and sometimes these actions can point to the complexity of a situation when multiple viewpoints are taken into account. However, since new information changes the context of the difficult ethical problem at hand, one can never think of the situation as being totally resolved. Rather, we prefer to think of it as working the situation and remaining open to change our assumptions, perceptions, and contexts as information becomes available.

Once actions are discerned and decided, then a new cycle of further inquiry can be initiated. The method progresses from description and reflection to action, and cycles back again. This leads us to the specific components of our method, which we give the acronym DIRR: description, interpretation, rehearsal, and rediscernment.

Description

As in qualitative research methods, the first step in working any ethical problem is description, which includes specifying the problem, providing its context, and identifying each individual's involvement, which Fesmire (2003) called "tangles of lived experience" (p. 28). Description is not only a singular activity but rather one in which multiple interpretations may be present. By fully describing the problem and reflecting upon one's personal involvement in it, individuals' values and beliefs will surface. This investigation could uncover deeply rooted values and beliefs about right and wrong, factors related to the cultural norms of the group, and habitual responses that are taken for granted.

What kinds of information should go into describing the dilemma? Include as much detail as possible, such as who is involved, what has occurred when and where, and so on. These details set the first stage of investigation before the next stage of analysis. Description is more about the facts as different stakeholders see them, and it behooves everyone to acknowledge that individual interpretations of the facts may vary considerably. This is where the leader's facilitation can be crucial. Acknowledging different perceptions and facilitating the sharing of them, the leader can start to uncover the complexity of the situation and possible resolutions to be considered.

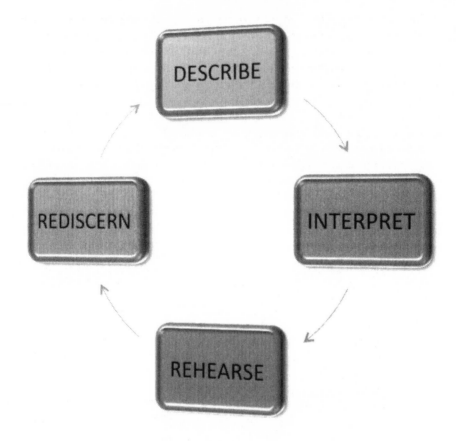

Figure 7.1.

We encourage the leader to strive toward describing the dilemma in as rich a language as possible, with each participant invited to contribute, not constrained to hold back. In the SPCO case, soliciting the emotional responses of the orchestra members, especially those invested with many years together, might draw out a richer, fuller description of events in light of needing a new musical director while meeting the SPCO's financial obligations.

It is also important to know where you as leader stand in the dilemma. Do you have vested interests in retaining what currently exists? Or do you support changing to another way or form? What do you stand to gain or lose in a particular resolution of the problem? Could your own values, beliefs, and opinions impede a fuller understanding of the situation? Do your current habits of mind influence or taint your reflections? For example, if you tend to value one person's views over another's, do that person's ideas overshadow others' views in this situation?

The action associated with the description phase is to ensure that each person involved has ample opportunity to comprehend varied points of view as fully as possible. This is where personal, introspective reflection becomes outward sharing and action. The leader seeks to account for all viewpoints as part of comprehensively investigating the problem.

This might involve setting up and facilitating processes that ensure participation by everyone, not only the dominant or influential few. It means including those who might be skeptical of changes or opposed to new developments. As Dewey pointed out, just because a certain viewpoint has become predominant, it does not mean that other viewpoints have necessarily disappeared. They may remain under the surface, re-emerging at the next available opportunity.

Key Questions in Description

1. Who is involved? What is their role, responsibility, and interest in the matter? What group(s) might they represent?
2. Are there organizational, institutional, or other habitual actions represented in the interests of those involved?
3. What has occurred and what were the consequences? What issues (e.g., academic, financial, social, political) are present?
4. What interests or viewpoints are at odds? Are there multiple perspectives presented? If not, why not? Is there already consensus on the matter?
5. Between the different sides of the problem, what are your initial leanings? Why? If you do not have a particular leaning in the situation, what accounts for that?
6. What are your empathies and sympathies as the leader? What leadership "blind spots" do these suggest to you?

Interpretation

The second phase of the method is analytical and interpretive, as it harnesses ethical language to assist in exploring the situation at hand. For our purposes, we shall encourage ethical interpretation, but there is no reason other interpretive lenses (e.g., economic, political, cultural) could not be used. The interpretive phase is significant because it raises individual habits, narrative judgments, and unconscious interpretations on the part of the participants in the situation. For the leader, this attempt to identify the actual ethical tensions involved and the institutional habits presented is critical to formulating possible resolutions to the problem.

Whether the situation is based on mutually exclusive beliefs among participants or groups is a key indication of the habits that may need to be faced in the situation. If one side feels that organizational rules must be upheld no matter the circumstances, whereas the other side considers rules as guidelines, not precepts, then an ethical tension exists between how rules are to be interpreted. If the situation is cast as either uphold the rules to the letter or interpret the rules as only guidelines, then the only possible outcome is winners and losers. There is no space in each side's interpretation for either context or strict adherence. Habits of fulfilling duty or desire leave little room for alternatives.

The problem with this type of approach is that no matter how strict one's interpretation of rules is, there will always be a time when strict interpretation is not adequate to the situation at hand. By the same token no matter how contextual one wishes to be in using rules as a guideline, there comes a point where rules are rules. The only way to surface the tension in a workable manner is to acknowledge through interpretation that such a tension exists.

Take, for example, the dispute that arose in a school that was seeking funding for smaller class sizes. The state government had defined a criterion related to poverty status in the student body that schools were required to meet to receive funds. The principal at one school found that by calculating absentees in one way, the school would be able to reduce class size by eight students per classroom. While legal, the method of calculation did not quite follow the letter of the law in meeting the specific requirements for the new funds. The ethical dilemma was whether to utilize such a formula to calculate student poverty toward the good end of smaller class sizes or to use the traditional formulas found in the rules governing the funds—utility versus duty.

Recall Dewey's identification of different ethical tensions. Is this a problem of social order involving hierarchy and authority? Is it a problem of change conflicts in which new ways are challenging more traditional ones? Are old and new ways mutually exclusive? To what extent is this a problem of private versus public interests? Who is most vested in each side of the argument? The questions help clarify the meaning of different arguments within ethical deliberation. Utilizing Dewey's ethical tensions (i.e., class and mass, old and new, private and public conflicts), the leader can seek further analytical intepretation to understand what is occurring.

Interpretation may seem overwhelming at first because of the complexity of the ethical situation. It may appear to stray from a straightforward resolution. Keep in mind that interpretation is not about reaching a singular agreement about solutions to the problem but rather about identifying, exploring, and even debating the underlying tensions present. We suggest that identifying behavioral habits combined with debating the merits of different ethical frames is helpful because the process can clarify issues and arguments made by the different sides. It can also encourage creativity and imagination in looking for viable next steps.

Key Questions in Interpretation

1. What are the ethical tensions represented by the problem? Is there tension between different universal beliefs held by members? Is it a question of what is virtuous for individual members versus what is virtuous for the group? Is it a question of utility versus duty?
2. Identify the habits of association present in the case. For example, are there habits of context versus habits of rule?
3. Are there problems of association in the case related to social order, change conflicts, or private versus public interests?
4. Has there been ample opportunity to discuss and debate the different ethical frameworks? Are there additional issues or concerns that have surfaced as a result?
5. Do the tensions imply possible actions by the leader or the group? If so, then move on to the rehearsal phase.

Rehearsal

Much like trying out different approaches to reading lines in a play, the rehearsal phase can allow for a closer tie-in to the information surfaced through description and the analytical lenses of interpretation. Dewey and Fesmire called this "dramatic rehearsal" because we do not act; rather we reflect upon the myriad of possibilities that might happen if a certain course of action is adopted. As much as possible, we play out the consequences that might occur as well as posit some unintended outcomes. Through rehearsal, we are in a better position to make a decision.

Rehearsal begins by hypothesizing the "what-ifs" of a situation before acting. We become more conscious of the possibilities, the true nature of the situation, and our own limitations in understanding the action that we might take. Having analyzed ethical tensions, we are better able to predict what might happen as we attend to our wants and desires as well as the duties and responsibilities of our leadership.

We take into account more of the complexity of satisfying competing ethics. For example, a school principal might want to purchase a new hands-on science curriculum offered by the district. In assessing the costs of implementing the curriculum, he realizes that the professional development funds for faculty might be in direct conflict with balancing the school budget and managing resources. Raising these ethical tensions, he could propose alternative resolutions that would balance the needs for professional development and fiscal responsibility.

The determinant of the best course of action should be the anticipated consequences that can be foreseen in consultation and collaboration with others. The strength of rehearsal in working an ethical problem is that the leader is asked to generate enough different solutions that something might emerge as a viable option.

We can also predict consequences based upon Dewey's problems of association by looking at social order, change conflicts, and private–public interests. For example, when the SPCO board members became aware of the financial situation for the chamber orchestra, they might have considered the implications of social ordering.

Suppose the players were designated according to a hierarchy, with some identified as essential to the orchestra and others considered expendable players who might be replaceable. The SPCO could retain only essential players, release expendable ones, and hire extras as needed at a much lower rate. If, however, the SPCO were more egalitarian, with musicans treated in the same way regardless of status, seniority, and specialty, then a possible solution might be to release all players. The result would be that the SPCO would no longer be a viable ensemble.

The action in the rehearsal phase both imagines possibilities and proposes actual courses of action. This can lead to better understanding the challenges associated with the situation. In the SPCO case, the board members eventually rejected the placement of musicians in a hierarchy because that would have compromised one of the most important things about chamber orchestras—the development of a tight ensemble sound that comes from a small group playing together over a period of time.

Considering the possible consequences of an action prepares participants for the next phase of working an ethical dilemma. For the SPCO, this involved determining the costs and benefits needed to retain the ensemble, calculating the demands on the group, considering the upset caused from player changes, and projecting the public's response to the orchestra's actions.

Key Questions in Rehearsal

1. What are possible alternative actions in working an ethical problem?
2. What might be intended and unintended consequences of those actions taken by the leadership and by others? How might others respond to the alternatives?
3. What actions might be deemed reasonable, feasible, or likely? What might be impossible to execute? Use of dramatic rehearsal could help answer these questions.
4. Are there metaphors, symbols, or other descriptors that might help participants understand the consequences of any one action?
5. Generate at least six different possible actions with their predicted consequences, even far-fetched ones. Are there any that consolidate the interests at hand or encourage improvement in the organization?

6. Once you have fully explored possible actions, what has become clearer for you or for the group? How do you imagine yourself and the group executing them?
7. What is your decision for resolution?

Rediscernment

Even though different possibilities have been explored and a decision has been made, the process is not yet complete. Dewey states that when one dips one's toe into a river and then does it again, be aware that the river water has changed. These changes require attention and an accounting in order to remain engaged in working the ethical problem. This is where rediscernment becomes important.

This phase involves discovering renewed energy for the challenge at hand through heightened awareness of the complexities, tensions, consequences, and likely possibilities of any given action. Rediscernment can break us out of the habitual language typically used to frame our approaches. It can encourage new ways to think about the problem and its resolution.

Language tools such as simile and metaphor may be applied to reframe the dilemma based upon the description and analysis already done. For example, using the metaphor of SPCO as family promotes a different set of options than considering it to be a for-profit business operation. Other creative techniques such as employing visualization and mind mapping can generate alternatives that might offer originality in meeting the needs of all involved. Thus, rediscernment brings an a priori quality of new understanding to the problem.

An acknowledgment of all points of view as part of rediscernment is important. This way, as new possibilities are articulated, the current context is honored. If the new possibility is not actually new but rather a reworking of an existing plan or strategy, then the context helps to identify why this might be the best choice.

Progress in working the ethical problem can come through its redefinition or redescription. For example, a person may experience racism in the workplace and be faced with how to deal with it. The decision could be whether to confront the individuals involved or turn a blind eye by ignoring what happened. While the situation may appear to be a very personal attack, the individual learns that it has happened to others in the organization, suggesting perpetuated group or institutional racism. Rediscerning this problem from "my personal problem" to a collective social concern in workplace racism fundamentally shifts the approach to the problem. It expands the scope of who might be involved, who might be affected, and the consequences for all.

Rediscernment calls for action that harmonizes interests and needs, assesses the consequences, indicates new actions for the group, and seeks to come out of the rhythm and harmony of the process so that there is a sense of grace that overlays the actions to be taken. We might not associate grace with the working of a major organizational dilemma. Nor do we often use terms such as harmony and rhythm. But there is a rhythm to conflict, wherein its very pulse waxes and wanes as new developments emerge.

Further, it is important that rediscernment not be confused with consensus or compromise. While consensus refers to the group's willingness to let a specific action move forward, the rediscernment phase is more about reaching a better understanding of the situation before any action is taken.

Compromise is generally thought of as finding the middle ground whereby people can agree, losing and winning something in the process. Differing from that, rediscernment seeks to build action out of a revised picture of the dilemma. There may be elements of compromise and consensus in this process, but ultimately the goal is a better understanding of the situation to enable resolution and action to be taken.

In part, the SPCO's financial problem was interwoven with the need for a new music director, the cost of which was a significant percentage of the SPCO's budget. However, when the players agreed to a pay cut, they helped the board members rediscern the problem and think differently about the directorship. Rather than retain the new music director, the board members chose to redefine that position as a revolving one, held by five highly respected musical consultants, such as violinist Joshua Bell and musician Bobby McFerrin, who would "consult" with the orchestra on programming and performance.

The SPCO board members saw this as an opportunity to develop the capacity of the ensemble while appealing to a broader audience than one director might be able to accomplish. And they could do so within the constraints of the SPCO's existing budget. The board members and the orchestra developed a way of collectively working through their problem that could increase their capacity to handle future challenges.

Finally, rediscernment may promote different organizational responses. A chamber orchestra used to having one music director will need to develop new ways to work with its five pro tempore consultants serving in the one position. In addition, communication of the new habits is enhanced by a clear description of what brought the group to the place where change became necessary in the first place. This means that the original dilemma, the process for working through it, and the new directions must be clearly communicated. This helps to work through the second-guessing that might take place and offers a new cultural interpretation for the SPCO to work with.

Key Questions in Rediscernment

1. What new understanding do you as leader have of the dilemma? To what extent does it address the interests of all concerned?
2. Are there different organizational and personal habits that may be required as you move forward with resolution of the dilemma? Would certain routines need to be modified or eliminated to satisfactorily work out the situation?
3. Is the original ethical problem coherently communicated in the plan to address it? What is needed to further clarify the problem?
4. To what extent are everyone's needs and interests accounted for so that there is at least tacit harmony in the organization?
5. Are there metaphors that might help to describe everyone's collective understanding of the situation? If so, what are these?

TOWARD A RESOLUTION

Often the resolution of an ethical problem appears to be correct, but this seeming correctness is more based upon the facts as we would like them to be rather than as they actually are. If possible, we need to approach ethical problems with an attitude of openheartedness, especially in considering our own assumptions and blind spots. Pragmatists recognize that applying certain principles, such as utilitarianism or virtue ethics, to a dilemma can be seductive because that can underscore our own views of the situation. Moreover, as we wrestle with ethical problems and related issues, it might be easier to draw upon past practice rather than attempt to engage in discernment and reflective action.

The DIRR method can enable us to be conscious of complex and sometimes conflicting data as people present them. If we are not mindful of the specific contexts, conflicts, and tensions as presented uniquely in specific situations, then we may arrive at a course of action that has nothing to do with the problem at hand.

Those with some background in organizational theory might recognize that we often rely upon familiar and tested strategies and actions regardless of the problem or dilemma. According to folk wisdom, "To the hammer, everything looks like a nail." So breaking through to new problem solving is definitely a challenge, but that is exactly the point of utilizing this method.

As stated before, if there is no real growth in the organization among individual participants or groups involved, then there is no chance of improvement and progress. This does not mean that previously held ideas should be summarily dismissed. Rather, in holding them to the same standard of examination that new information is generally subjected, we believe that leaders have more possibility to work the problems in a meaningful way.

SPCO ENCORE

Unfortunately much of the creativity experienced in the 2004–2005 negotiations was gone by 2011. The board members proclaimed a bleak financial picture for the orchestra that while realistic did not leave much room for the musicians to offer their own perspective. Consequently, negotiations became more and more strident and less about a collective understanding of the situation at hand, and contract talks between players and management broke down. In October 2011, the board members made the unprecedented decision to lock out their professional musicians, resulting in cancellation of the 2011–2012 SPCO season. It wasn't until May 2013 that the musicians and the board members settled their differences and agreed to a contract. Lost in over a year of lockout was the creativity and goodwill that was a hallmark of the SPCO. Unfortunately, the long dispute resulted in the loss of several key musicians. At the time of this writing, a new board chair seeks to recreate the SPCO of old while acknowledging the hubris of the lockout.

The case demonstrates that organizational leadership is dynamic and always evolving. As illustrated, this dynamism can be a step back from the moral imagination and creativity required to keep the finances of such an organization healthy. We do not suggest that had the board members and musicians of the SPCO applied the method suggested in this book they might be in a different place. But we have observed that when presented with the same problem in 2004, the first resolution was far more collective and creative. The dynamics of leadership can be in support of a growth model or a model that discourages growth. The DIRR is meant to encourage dynamic, moral creativity toward institutional growth.

SUMMARY

Informed by the work of Dewey and Fesmire, our inquiry method for ethical deliberation seeks to be useful and pragmatic for leaders. The criteria to determine its utility are that it is exploratory, dynamic, imaginative, and capacity building. The SPCO's dilemma illustrates how the process of discernment and action work together in the four phases of the DIRR method: description, interpretation, rehearsal, and rediscernment. While appearing to be serial, the method progresses from description to reflection and cycles back as new information or insight occurs. But there are no easy answers or simple resolutions that ensure success for the organization.

Through the process, you would have engaged all parties and considered their perspectives as much as possible. You would remain open, creative, and discerning. While one solution might not necessarily be ideal and some might disagree with the course of action taken, you can remain open to reflection and reconsideration. You should not feel compromised or that you have given too much away. By proposing the DIRR method, we hope you are better prepared to act progressively in ways that are mutually beneficial to the individuals as well as to the organization as a whole.

III

Applications

EIGHT

Education Cases to Consider

Educational leaders often regard their ethical decisions in practical terms. Prudently, they investigate the details of the situation along with determining the appropriate action to be taken. They consider antecedent factors and weigh consequences relating to the outcomes desired from the actions. There might be state and federal regulations that stipulate certain requirements for achievement, management, funding, and compliance. Leaders may need to examine very firmly held personal or professional values, perhaps in direct conflict with others to whom they are accountable. These make for ethical dilemmas in deciding right action and good outcomes.

In this chapter, we present nine cases that illustrate various kinds of conflicts that demand ethical decision making. Each case is briefly described and then presented in greater detail. Readers may wish to go through all of the cases or selectively choose ones of more interest or relevance. Apply the DIRR method—description, interpretation, rehearsal, and rediscernment—by considering the general, as well as specific, questions to each case.

Begin by considering the extent to which the information provided is adequate. Do you as a reader know who the key players are in the case? Is the primary decision maker different from the administrator in charge? Are there contextual factors related to the specific school or locale that might be relevant to resolving the case?

For example, in a student truancy case, the location of the school and its multi-ethnic student body factored into how students were treated differently. This kind of background information may be necessary to consider. Another case involving a similar attendance problem but situated in a different school might generate a different set of issues or concerns.

What are the legal, ethical, and moral issues in the case? Discriminating between actions that are deemed legal and illegal is different from deciding what might be a good thing to do or the right action to take. In a case about employee conduct, the key decision maker was the supervisor who was determining whether to reprimand the employee for inappropriate conduct. Some key issues in that case involved due process in handling personnel matters, treating all employees fairly, and determining appropriate conduct in an educational setting.

If the decision maker were a fellow employee rather than the supervisor, the dilemma might involve different issues, like speaking truthfully about the situation or remaining loyal to one's colleague. Rather than due process and fair treatment, the case might be more personal in nature and involve considering what individual values are most pressing.

What additional information would be helpful in the case? Perhaps certain school policies or laws might be needed to clarify regulations and legal aspects of the case. Has this situation ever occurred in the school district? What has been the policy in the past? Are there legal rules that bind what action should be taken? Might a specialist or legal consultant be able to assist? Should further investigation occur before action is taken?

Could other individuals besides the leader be involved in the decision making? For example, in a case involving a teacher, principal, and superintendent, the decision varies if it were placed in the hands of the school principal or the top system-level administrator. Reconsidering who is responsible to whom broadens the perspectives considered as well as the consequences for people involved in the case.

There are additional concerns if we must think about implications for administration beyond the classroom, or even beyond the school building. Suppose the governing body is the school board. How might ethical deliberation be considered if it must be negotiated among various members of a diverse school board? What is the relationship between the school superintendent and the school board?

If other key actors are involved in the case, try to account for their perspectives. Japanese filmmaker Akira Kurosawa depicted three versions of an incident in the film *Rashomon*, stringing one version after the other and allowing the viewers to conclude who was telling the truth. Changing one's perspective is a useful means for balancing the perspective of the primary decision maker with others who might play key roles in the situation. This strategy takes the primary decision maker out of the drama, allowing some distance and perhaps objectivity. It can illumine alternatives, which might not have been available initially.

The general questions aligned with the DIRR method are listed in Table 8.1. These may be useful in working the ethical dilemmas and probing more deeply the conflicts that might underlie the situation at hand.

CASES IN ELEMENTARY AND SECONDARY EDUCATION

Case 1: Choosing a New Principal

Synopsis

To fill the vacancy for principal at Pacific Heights Elementary School, Superintendent Feinstein appointed a five-member committee to conduct a search and interview candidates. Of the three possibilities, the first choice of the committee is not the superintendent's choice. Her preferred candidate was ranked third by the committee. With no time for another search, what should the superintendent do?

Detailed Narrative

For Superintendent Kate Feinstein, choosing a new principal for Pacific Heights Elementary School will not be easy. The individual appointed must turn around a chronically underperforming school with low student achievement, poor attendance, and high teacher turnover. The problems have been so long-standing that the most recent principal lasted only six months. Because the school failed to meet benchmarks for the past three years, it will be heavily monitored. Whoever is selected to be principal must take on the problems while Feinstein closely supervises the reform process.

The superintendent appointed a five-member search committee made up of two principals, a teacher, a curriculum resources person, and a parent. The committee was directed to review applications, interview the top candidates, and make its recommendations to Superintendent Feinstein. With an applicant pool of only three candidates, the committee chose to interview all three.

The first candidate, Allison Steiner, was curriculum coordinator at a nearby high school. Despite having only secondary school experiences, she has an impressive background in curriculum and instruction, potentially bringing the necessary academic rigor to improve test scores. However, during her interview, she came off sounding like a know-it-all. According to the curriculum resource person serving on the search committee, "Ms. Steiner's very competent in her area, but that's secondary school curriculum, not elementary. I wonder if she can handle the lower grades." It was also reported that while in her current position, Allison had created unrest among the faculty with a union grievance filed against her. A teacher on the committee had heard about this incident. But was it merely gossip?

Second to be interviewed was Paul Talisman, a second-grade teacher new to the district and just finishing his principal licensure program. Although well meaning, he did not have the requisite skills and experi-

Table 8.1.   DIRR Questions

DIRR Method	Key Elements	Questions
Description	Problem Key persons Sequence of events Issues, concerns Interests represented	What appears to be the problem that needs resolution? Who is involved? What are their roles, responsibilities, or interest in the matter? What occurred and when? Are there individual or group interests in this situation? Do certain individuals represent specific groups?

Interpretation	Duties based	*Sources of ethical tension*
	Desires based	What is the right action
	Virtue ethics	based on rules or duties?
	Group or societal ethics	To what extent do the
	Social order conflicts	leader's duties bind her or
	Old versus new	him to a specific course of
	Private versus public	action?
		What is in the best interest
		of the majority? What are
		utilitarian concerns?
		What constitutes good
		leadership? To what extent
		does one's personal and
		professional life contribute
		to making an ethical
		decision?
		What constitutes "good" for
		the group or society?
		Does social order (e.g.,
		who responds to whom,
		who is related to whom)
		need to be considered in
		resolving this case? Is
		there a hierarchical
		relationship (e.g.,
		employee to supervisor) or
		dominant group involved in
		the case?
		Are there traditional views
		or customs that are being
		challenged by new or
		different ones?
		How do private interests
		clash with public concerns?
		Is this a private matter, or
		does it involve public
		interests?
Rehearsal	Consequences	What might be some
		possible actions and likely
		consequences? Are there
		unintended consequences
		that might occur?
		What are some short-term
		outcomes or long-term
		outcomes from the actions
		to be taken?

| Rediscernment | Timetable reframing
Inclusiveness
Reassessment | What language tools (e.g., simile, metaphor) or creative techniques (e.g., visualization, mind mapping) could be used in reframing the problem?
As much as possible, have all viewpoints been included and given due consideration in resolving the situation?
Have new information and insight helped redefine the problem? Is there a revision of the dilemma? |

ence, as evidenced by his application and the vague responses given during the interview. It seemed unlikely that he could lead an underperforming school. The committee felt that Paul had potential and might make a good principal someday, but not right now and not at Pacific Heights.

The third candidate was Mary Jo McCarthy, a personable special education teacher from another elementary school. Like a doting grandmother, Mrs. McCarthy charmed the committee with her manner. Even though she was being interviewed, she passed around cookies and tea as if in her own home. She definitely had a calming effect, important if she was to work with an admittedly tough faculty. But could she lead the school in reform? Her knowledge of curriculum was limited. She didn't understand how to read data about student achievement and yearly progress. One principal on the search committee expressed these reservations as follows:

> It's likely Mary Jo will retire soon. Should we risk Pacific Heights on someone who will be out soon? But maybe the school needs someone short term to heal the wounds among the faculty. Mrs. McCarthy could do that.

Aware that they were making a recommendation to the superintendent, the committee became seriously invested in advocating for Mrs. McCarthy. All members felt that she could learn what she lacked. The other two candidates were not deemed adequate to the task—Paul because he lacked sufficient experience and Allison because she lacked elementary school background as well as interpersonal skills.

Superintendent Kate Feinstein had doubts, wondering about Mrs. McCarthy's qualifications and motivation. If Mary Jo had been interested in gaining curriculum knowledge, she would have done so by now. And, yes, she was close to retirement age, and income from a principalship would certainly boost her salary. Regardless of her motivation, how would Mary Jo handle curriculum matters?

Allison Steiner seemed the most knowledgeable in curriculum and assessment to lead Pacific Heights out of its restructured status. But the committee raised important concerns about her communication skills. Some of the committee members had gotten to know Allison through the synagogue that they attended. Would their choosing Allison be seen as a biased choice?

What about the second candidate, Paul Talisman? Was he a more viable alternative than the other two? With school scheduled to start in ten days and no time for conducting another search, Feinstein needed to appoint a principal for Pacific Heights as soon as possible. What should she do?

Additional Questions to Consider

1. Good selection: Selecting the right leader is important. How important are the candidate's background knowledge, skills, and experience? What about personal relationships and communication skills?
2. Individual versus group: Is the superintendent obligated to the committee or vice versa? What might be the immediate as well as long-term consequences from this decision?
3. Utilitarianism: From a utilitarian argument, how can the superintendent maximize the good for the school and the district in choosing a new principal?
4. Compromise candidate: Is there a way to appoint someone whom both the committee and the superintendent might agree upon? Would Paul Talisman be a viable alternative?
5. Sources of information: To what extent should the superintendent rely on prior information such as knowing the individual outside of the professional setting? How does one use information that might be hearsay or gossip?

Case 2: Cyberbullying

Synopsis

An Arab American student tells his guidance counselor that he has received extremely mean comments about his being a Muslim that were made repeatedly in an online social networking site. He does not want to provide the names of the students he believes are behind the cyberbullying. Because there is no school policy or official directive about it, there has been nothing to protect him from these actions. As the guidance counselor, what could you do?

Detailed Narrative

At Edison High School, a science and technology magnet school, the "best and the brightest" students from all over the city compete to be placed there in their freshman year. Among the new freshman class are a handful of Arab Americans who have come across town to enter this school because of its outstanding STEM program. Not only are there interesting projects in robotics, human genetics, and physics taught by an outstanding faculty but also grants, resources, and college scholarships for those who successfully complete Edison's rigorous secondary math and science curriculum.

By contrast, 60 percent of the student body of the other high school, Albertson High, is of Arabic descent, some who have lived in the United States for several generations and have assimilated into American culture. There were also those more recently emigrated from Syria, Lebanon, Yemen, Iran, and Iraq. Because of the special needs of these students, there is little by way of resources dedicated to gifted and talented students, much less those who have an interest and aptitude for mathematics and science.

Further, over the past decade, a more vocal Arab American community has evolved, uniting those of more conservative Muslim backgrounds. In part, this was due to the increased attention and negative publicity against Arabic speakers, specifically Muslims. The Arab American community united to support its members in acculturating to a new country as well as to fight off negative stereotypes directed against Muslims.

A recent admission to Edison High School, Ahmad Hussein is a gifted freshman who successfully competed to enter the high school and appears to be doing exceptionally well in his first semester. He is a gentle, quiet young man who appears to love mathematics and thrives at the school. But in early December, he came in to see the school guidance counselor. He confided that in the past month there have been extremely mean comments made to him as a Muslim as well as some serious threats made to his safety at Edison, all posted anonymously online. He does not want to provide any names of the students who might be behind this cyberbullying.

Investigating these allegations, the counselor finds that there is evidence that Ahmad has been the victim of cyberbullying. The threats have been mean-spirited, cruel, and nasty. His teachers have noted that his behavior seems to have been affected negatively and his classwork has suffered.

Edison High School requires the use of the Internet as a homework tool, but there is no official directive or policy on how to use the technology properly. Many of the teachers believe that cyber etiquette and ethics instruction would cut into too much valuable instructional time in the core academic areas that are important to succeed on state and national achievement testing. None of the cyberbullying had previously occurred at Edison, and there are no cyberbullying policies in the school system that might protect Ahmad or any other student.

Recently the cyberbullying seems to have intensified, and Ahmad appears more despondent. He has come in to ask about transferring back to Albertson High School, where he might feel more "protected" and safe. One of the teachers in his STEM program suggested this option to him and encouraged this for his own safety. Likewise, the department chair suggested that keeping silent on the matter would be best, as this cyberbullying incident might incite the local Arab American community to take action. Knowing Ahmad's potential, the school counselor is reluctant to be silent, as Edison High can offer this very talented and gifted young man so much more for a career in mathematics.

Additional Questions to Consider

1. Leadership: Who needs to take action in this matter? How might the counselor involve the principal or other leaders to protect students like Ahmad?
2. Individual versus group: Is this a problem of one student or the group of Arab American students? Could this be a school-wide problem that requires a general policy to deter future action?
3. Knowledge to take action: Many teachers feel ill equipped to prevent cyberbullying or have little cyber safety knowledge. What might be done about this at Edison?
4. Religious freedom: To what extent must there be tolerance and religious freedom extended in this situation? Who is authorized to make that determination?
5. Equal educational opportunity: Is there an issue of equal educational opportunity in this case? If so, what provisions are being made to ensure that there is equal opportunity?

Case 3: Personal Matter

Synopsis

A charming and charismatic department chair is rumored to have had numerous affairs with faculty members at school. However, that has not reflected in his performance on the job, and the principal has tended to ignore what were deemed "personal matters." Recently, the principal hired a twenty-eight-year-old science teacher who is attractive and somewhat naive. The department chair is making advances that border on being inappropriate and out of line. Should the principal step in?

Detailed Narrative

Tad McCutcheon had been at Heritage High for nearly fifteen years, serving for the past decade as the science department chair. During that time, his charismatic leadership had made people take notice of what was occurring there. Over the years, student achievement in science had shot through the roof. Science fair awardees were numerous; special recognition was given to competitive placements in the robotics and engineering competitions at the state level. Students were recognized for their projects in the National Youth Science Camp. The school even had two winning entries in the International Science and Engineering Competition held last year.

No question, this department chair was responsible for these accomplishments. He was definitely a mover. Not only did his own students excel, but anyone taking a science course had done better than most schools in the district. McCutcheon was more than just a good teacher; he was a visionary leader who could move his department ahead of the pack.

Tad was also tall, dark, and very handsome, with a classical Mediterranean profile. He seemed to be a natural-born athlete, very energetic, and competitive in tennis and golf. At forty, he was still single and was thought to be a very eligible bachelor. Women teachers at Heritage not only found him charming, but it was rumored that he had had numerous affairs with several faculty members.

These rumors had not troubled Principal Norman Santos in the past. He had hired Tad and had seen how the young man matured from a "kid wet behind the ears" to a competent and charismatic leader of the Science Department and also of Heritage High. There was no question that he was excellent. Was it Tad's fault that he was also good looking and that he attracted women like flies? Norman chose to let consenting adults do what they did as long as it didn't interfere with school morale and student achievement. His view was that this was a personal matter and that there should be freedom of choice.

But the current situation seemed different. Mr. Santos had recently hired a new teacher for the Science Department, Leah Plushenko, a twenty-eight-year-old who had been a biologist doing research for several years before returning for teacher certification. A Russian by birth, she and her family had immigrated to the United States when she was just twelve. While she seemed to be Western in most ways, there appeared to be an "old country" way about her. At times, she seemed younger than her years and more naive than most in handling students. Blond and petite, she seemed so tiny compared to the juniors and seniors in her classes.

As Science Department chair, McCutcheon was her immediate supervisor and had been willing to go the extra mile to make sure that she succeeded as a science teacher. They seemed to get along well, and his help appeared to ease her transition into teaching at Heritage High. Tad would often stop by during lunch or after school to talk about lessons and how her teaching was going. When asked about her progress, he reported that she was "doing just fine."

One night after a parent–teacher meeting, Mr. Santos noticed lights still on in Ms. Plushenko's biology lab. It was after 10 p.m., and that seemed pretty late for a school night. Passing by the classroom, he noticed two silhouettes huddled close together. "None of my business," he muttered to himself.

The next afternoon at the faculty meeting, Mr. Santos had faculty members working in smaller breakout groups by their respective departments. Walking around the room, he noticed that Tad was leading the discussion in the Science Department group. Seated next to him was a red-faced Leah Plushenko, who seemed uncomfortable and somewhat fidgety. As Norman Santos walked by the group, he noticed that Tad had his hand on Leah's thigh while he was talking. The other faculty in the group didn't seem to notice. "Is this any of my business?" Santos wondered. But Leah sure did look young. After all, she was the same age as Norman's own daughter.

Additional Questions to Consider

1. Rules, regulations, and guidelines: How would you as administrator determine whether there was a sexual encounter in this case? What rules and regulations currently exist in your school organization to offer guidance? Once determined, are you obligated to act?
2. Determining faculty conduct: What determines good conduct on the part of faculty? How does this apply to those with supervisory responsibilities such as department chairpersons and administrators?
3. Social order conflicts: To what extent does the hierarchical relationship between the teacher and her department chair need to be taken into account? Is it relevant to deciding what to do?
4. Private versus public considerations: Is this a private affair or does the case have consequences for the school community as a whole? What might be some unintended consequences in this case?

Case 4: Homecoming

Synopsis

Homecoming at Tranquil Bay High is full of tradition and specific rituals such as the practice of hazing sophomore classmates. This case illustrates the dilemma of an administrative intern attempting to retain specific cultural activities associated with the celebration while curbing the violence that has been escalating against students.

Detailed Narrative

Like most high schools in the United States, homecoming at Tranquil Bay High School is full of tradition. Alumni are invited back to attend school functions and reacquaint themselves with the community. Students participate in a week of friendly competition among the grade levels to build school identity and nurture a sense of belonging. At half-time during a football game with a school rival, the king and queen of homecoming are crowned along with a court of princes and princesses. After the game, the students attend a dance or other social to build school spirit.

However, Tranquil Bay homecoming activities in recent years have included hazing the sophomores. While the practice was illegal in the state, it appeared to be getting more malicious at Tranquil Bay. Last year, on the Thursday night of homecoming week, juniors and seniors went on an all-night rampage of vandalism, writing obscene messages on teachers' cars and homes. Several sophomores were apparently "kidnapped" and duct-taped to stop signs in town. Other captured boys were publicly humiliated in public nudity or other demeaning activities. Several girls who were kidnapped reported being sexually and physically harassed.

Afterward, school administrators were inundated with calls from parents about the incidents but turned the matter over to the local police. This was also an unmitigated disaster, as an editorial in the local paper questioned "What do we pay administrators for?"

The following year, the administration considered canceling homecoming altogether, but because community outcry was so great, they recanted. While those who were negatively affected by the hazing were clamoring for changes in homecoming week, many vested in the old traditions, as well as the community at large, placed a great deal of pressure on the school to continue all the traditions and activities. So the administrators had an ethical dilemma on their hands.

Principal Harold Spencer decided to give the problem to a newly appointed administrative intern, Shelly Sakamoto. She had been an English teacher at Tranquil Bay and later department chair for a number of years. Her familiarity with the high school and community would be a plus. Spencer realized that it was a tough assignment for a novice administrator, but at present he could not spare his other assistant principals for this thorny assignment.

When given the assignment, Shelly wondered why past administrative interventions to control the hazing had not worked. Recommended solutions were based on information gleaned by administration. Teachers had not been asked, nor had they volunteered any ideas toward a solution. The students were consulted only after the fact, and the community was not invited for input either through informal means such as coffee hours to discuss the matter or through more formal contacts with the local police and city offices.

Changes failed to curb the maliciousness, and the administrators felt isolated as well as frustrated by the problem. Basically, they resigned themselves to a week that would be, in Principal Spencer's words, "just another one of life's trials." But an assistant principal said, "If this community doesn't wake up soon, some kid is going to get killed."

Reflecting on the problem, Shelly realized that her own empathies in the situation were influenced by wanting to do a good job while not making the administrative team look bad for not having provided meaningful solutions and taken care of the problem. As an administrative intern, did she even have the political clout to implement a solution while others with more experience had failed so miserably?

Additional Questions to Consider

1. Duties and desires: What is the right action to take, and what good outcomes might be desirable in resolving the problem?
2. Moral, ethical, and legal concerns: If hazing is illegal in the state, what are some legal issues or concerns to be considered? Should these be dealt with differently than ethical or moral issues? Why or why not?
3. Utilitarianism: What is best for the school as a whole, and who should determine that? Who needs to be involved in the deliberation and solution?
4. Preserving traditions: Are there values that the school might want to retain and reinforce during this homecoming celebration? At what cost should traditions and customs be retained?
5. Authority: Does Shelly, the administrative intern, have sufficient authority to make a decision in this case? If not, what course of action might she take?

Case 5: Academic Freedom

Synopsis

Usually the administration sends out "good news" notices and information to everyone through its social media and Twitter accounts. This is generally thought to be the best way to communicate uniformly to the school community. This case illustrates how one tweet could ignite a barrage of comments despite the individual teacher's desire to send a restricted message to her department colleagues.

Detailed Narrative

Soraya didn't realize how one little e-link could create such a stir. Actually, when she first sent it out, there was hardly a ripple. It seemed to be an important statement for all social justice advocates seeking peace among divergent splinter groups. The e-link about LGBT issues had been from a colleague at another school and was being circulated by friends in the social justice network across the state. For those who might be interested, there was a contact person and suggestions for supporting the peace and social justice network. Soraya figured that those who were interested could email to the e-link, while those who were opposed could simply delete the link. So she added a note of her personal endorsement and clicked the Send button to forward the tweet to her colleagues at school.

Unfortunately, the unintended consequence was that the school sent a Twitter message out to the entire school community. The purpose of the Twitter account was to share the "good news" from the high school on a regular basis to keep students, teachers, parents, and community informed. Soraya accidently sent her tweet to that account, and the response was swift and very negative.

"Who the hell is sending this trash to our students!"

"I find any propagandizing offensive."

"Trash stuff unrelated to my job."

"Delete my name from this account."

At that point, the electronic barrage started attracting those defending Soraya's statement for peace and her use of the school's social media and the Twitter account to say so. School faculty and staff, even students, parents, and the community folks, all began sending messages back and forth.

Some supported the link, especially LGBT advocates. Others criticized tweeting about social justice concerns and nonacademic issues on the school's Twitter account. Other messages started targeting Soraya personally on her LGBT leanings and preferences. The tweets were hardly substantive and most were negative. Soraya was beginning to wonder about her Lincoln Middle School colleagues with whom she had spent the past decade.

Additional Questions to Consider

1. Academic freedom and free speech: Is the proper use of a school's social media and Twitter accounts for information only on approved communication? To omit politics, foreign policy, or religion amounts to censorship, doesn't it? Should there be restricted access? What are the boundaries?

2. Decision maker: What is the administrator's responsibility? Can the administrator shut down the account and place sanctions against users? If so, what is the recourse to this action from those who have been silenced?
3. Communication: How does having e-communication challenge existing modes to connect and communicate with each other?
4. Acceptable behavior: What about net etiquette? What is acceptable e-communication behavior on a school's account? Who should be monitoring it?

Case 6: Career Interference

Synopsis

Having established a strong leadership team, Principal Allan Freire might lose his talented assistant principal, Janelle Wright. The superintendent has told him of a principalship opening the third year of Janelle's contract. If Allan grants permission for her to break her contract, the superintendent has made clear that the job will be hers. What should Principal Freire do?

Detailed Narrative

As principal of Crispus Attucks High School, Allan Freire recruited an excellent leadership team to boost student achievement. Janelle Wright is the assistant principal in charge of instruction for whom he negotiated a three-year contract at premium salary. Considered an outstanding teacher trainer statewide, Janelle helped the high school teachers individualize their approach to language arts so that their teaching could become more student centered.

In August, before the new school year was to open, Principal Freire received an email from the superintendent:

> Banneker Elementary is opening next year and I really need a good principal there. I was thinking Janelle has the necessary administrative experience and your faculty has been singing her praises. Of course, I wouldn't poach her if you feel she should stay at Attucks since she's under contract. But I'd really like to post her at Banneker.

Allan had wanted to avoid this kind of situation when he negotiated these three-year contracts. In the past, the district had taken fairly new assistant principals like Janelle and placed them in principalships to either sink or swim. Freire advocated for a longer training period to support leadership development and create stability in schools. Specifically, he negotiated three-year contracts for his two assistant principals to ensure that they remain at the high school.

His first hire was Assistant Principal Don Potter, who took over daily school monitoring and management. Don collected data on aspects such as lunch discipline, absenteeism, and parent contacts to predict where student support might be needed. His greatest strength was in number crunching and data management, not people skills. Allan frequently had to mediate between Potter and the office staff, but that was worthwhile given Don's analytical expertise.

Janelle Wright was Potter's opposite. Personable and genuinely likable, she knew about teaching kids and could motivate teachers. Once hired at the high school, she began conducting teaching observations and individual meetings with all faculty, even the most resistant ones. By the end of the first term, Janelle had helped each teacher diagnose numerous ways to differentiate instruction in the classroom. She established a peer-review system that promoted teachers learning from each other through mentoring and coaching. Her work as instructional leader was beginning to show in terms of student achievement.

Last year, Attucks's test scores improved slightly but not enough to get the school off annual yearly progress (AYP) status. Over the summer, the leadership team had used Potter's data analysis and Wright's teaching diagnoses to devise a comprehensive yet workable school improvement plan. Freire was excited to see how the school would fare with routines in place, benchmarks set, and teachers supported to achieve the targets. With another year to work the plan, Crispus Attucks High could really take off.

Losing Janelle at this time would set the school back at least a year, maybe two. The high school was a place that needed stability and commitment to ensure change. Losing a leadership team member would be a severe blow to efforts at building relationships and sustaining change. Anyway, by the time Janelle was free of her three-year commitment to Crispus Attucks, there would be other principal vacancies available, and she could easily get one of them.

On the other hand, Janelle did want to become a principal someday, managing a school in her own coaching and mentoring style. Allan would be proud if she joined the principal ranks in the district. Maybe she should be told of the vacancy at Banneker. After all, she was not young, having spent many years in staff development and only now entering administration. Her husband had recently retired, so who knew how long she would want to remain in the school district? Yes, he felt that he could train another person to step into the assistant principal's position; after all, he had done it before.

Here was Allan's dilemma. What was good for Janelle seemed to be at odds with the school's needs, and what was good for the school seemed to get in the way of Janelle's career path. What should Principal Freire do?

Additional Questions to Consider

1. Decision maker: Whose decision is this? Is it right for the principal to interfere with Janelle's career? Is the principal obligated to follow the superintendent's request? Is it ethical for the superintendent to place Allan in this position?
2. One versus the many: Are the needs of the many (the students at Attucks School) more important in this case than the needs of the one (Assistant Principal Janelle Wright)?
3. Moral, ethical, and legal concerns: What are the moral, ethical, and legal considerations in breaking an employment contract?
4. Virtues: What values (e.g., truth, loyalty, responsibility, caring) might guide the principal's deliberation and decision making?
5. Old versus new clashes: To what extent is Allan seeking stability in his school while opposing change in leadership?

CASES IN HIGHER EDUCATION

In this second edition, we wanted to honor the request of our students for cases that might be related to higher education issues and concerns. We offer these additional cases, presented briefly for review and consideration.

Case 7: Faculty Recommendation

Synopsis

A department chair must choose between two potential candidates in a faculty search that pits a well-regarded faculty member against a newly minted scholar, both committed to Native Americans in higher education. Who is to be recommended to the dean?

Detailed Narrative

As the department chair of a newly instituted language/culture program honoring indigenous peoples, you are excited about the prospect of hiring a faculty member to spearhead this effort. From the applicant pool, the search committee has forwarded two names for consideration. The first applicant is well known for his longtime commitment to native peoples and their culture, having taught for many years at the local community college. He is now hoping to secure a position at the flagship university campus. Though not a native himself, he has demonstrated his knowledge and competence in the language. He might not be flashy, but he is steady and reliable.

The second applicant is an up-and-coming scholar with an impressive curriculum vitae from a top-notch research institution. She would be the first Native American appointed to this university. But she is also a young scholar, inexperienced at teaching and program development. Your dean favors having this rising star, but the search committee members are split in their recommendations. The faculty members who met with both applicants expressed their preferences for either the more experienced community college faculty member or the rising star. Your dilemma as department chair is whom to recommend to the dean, and your voice could be the tiebreaker.

Additional Questions to Consider

1. Factors for consideration: What factors must be considered in comparing the two candidates? For example, how might tenure considerations, rank at appointment, salary, and other variables play in making the hiring decision? Should these factors influence your recommendation as department chair?
2. Valuing diverse perspectives: What might each prospective candidate bring to a newly instituted program? Whose perspectives (individual and/or group) are honored if the department recommends one person over the other?
3. Problems of association: With the department split on its recommendation, how might you ensure that a recommendation does not result in resentment or negative consequences for interdepartmental relationships?
4. Hierarchy: Are there potential issues in dealing with the dean if the appointment goes against his or her desires? If you follow what the dean wants, how might this play out in the department among the faculty?

Case 8: Fast Track Administrator

Synopsis

Serving on a college-wide committee to reassess programs for the dean, you realize that your own program does not look very good. In particular, your program is deficient in several key areas, and your immediate supervisor appears at fault. The consequences for your program might be very negative. But shouldn't you take the wider view of the whole college? How do you report and respond to the dean?

Detailed Narrative

You are a relatively new administrator who is on the fast track in your school/university organization. Your dean must reorganize and prioritize all educational programs in the organization. Your immediate supervisor has asked that you assist directly in the effort by serving on a college-wide committee and report to the dean.

You want to do a good job in assessing your own program's performance, but the consequences might mean that you would rate your program low because it has not reflected the overall organization's mission and goals. It has also been inefficient in a number of key areas (staffing, performance, internal vs. external needs). Should you report accordingly, it could mean that staff would be cut, aspects of the program might be curtailed, and your immediate supervisor would not look good. She has headed the program for at least a decade, and improvements to the existing program have been minimal.

Could an honest assessment in reporting the data make everyone else in the unit look poorly? As the administrator in charge of this section, you could also remain silent, but that would mean that there would be no changes in program or curriculum. The status quo has not been beneficial especially to underrepresented minority students in the program. What should you do?

Additional Questions to Consider

1. Duties versus desires: Are you clear about your duties in this case that might direct you toward taking a particular action? What might be the best interests for the majority?
2. Working the tension: How might you handle the political fallout of truthful reporting and unraveling the status quo? Are you aware of the consequences, both likely and unintended from your actions?
3. Truth versus loyalty: Is there a place for loyalty in this case? Do you owe your supervisor your loyalty, or should you be directed toward institutional improvement?
4. Inclusiveness: Have all points of view been taken into account? Might you need to investigate further? If so, with whom might you consult?

Case 9: Required Reading

Synopsis

The required reading for the campus was a scholarly work about the Koran, which in itself was a very controversial choice made by a committee of students, faculty, and administrators. Should you support this selection, or might you advocate for an alternative choice for faculty and students?

Detailed Narrative

In May, all incoming students, freshmen primarily and transfer students, were told to read an assigned book over the summer in preparation for a college-wide seminar series at the opening of the school year. The book that was selected by a committee of students, faculty, and administrators was a scholarly work about the Koran (also spelled Qur'an), the Islamic text that lays out the principles of that religion. The purpose of the selection was to enable Americans to read and discuss an influential text relevant to human history.

In preparing for the upcoming seminars, students were asked to write a one-page response to one of the chapters of the Koran as presented in the book. Those who chose not to respond were allowed to write a one-page essay explaining their objections. Attendance at the event was not taken, nor were assignments to be graded.

Most students showed up, however, and the faculty led small-group discussions. The two-hour seminars took place despite a Christian group's attempt to block the discussions through a federal lawsuit. Clearly, reading this required text and holding the two-hour seminars created controversy at the university, and you have been placed in the uncomfortable position of defending this curricular decision. How might you deal with the consequences, both intended and unintended, resulting from this required reading assignment?

Additional Questions to Consider

1. Democratic ethics: As an administrator on the college campus, would you support these seminars? Why or why not?
2. Sufficient information: What additional information might be helpful to decide? What educational principles are at stake?
3. Leadership: Would it matter what position you held at the college, whether you support or oppose this kind of activity? Does social order (who reports to whom) need to be considered in this case?
4. Outcomes: Are there long-term as well as short-term consequences that might be relevant? What about any unintended consequences that could result?

SUMMARY

In this chapter, six cases in K–12 education and three cases in higher education settings were presented for the reader's consideration. Each case included a synopsis, a detailed narrative, and some discussion questions. While some of the cases were event specific, all suggested a historical context that we hope encourages the reader to dig deeper and probe more rigorously. Unlike case narratives that present problems and offer solutions, we invite the reader to consider personal as well as professional reactions and propose resolutions that derive from the inquiry. Our experience is that ethical problems do not simply get resolved; rather, they require an iterative process that can evolve as one's knowledge and skills increase.

NINE

More Cases to Consider

Deborah DeMeester, Ed.D.,
University of St. Thomas

Leaders in many different contexts face ethical situations in their work as well as in their personal lives. In this chapter, we present cases outside of the realm of education that require ethical decision making. Each case is presented in synopsis and then described in greater detail. Feel free to selectively choose cases that may be of interest. Consider how the DIRR method might be applied to explore describing, interpreting, rehearsing and rediscerning what is occurring. Refer back to Table 8.1 for general questions on the method. In addition, there are some added considerations related to the specific cases presented.

PERSONAL CASES

Case 1: Maximizing Value

Synopsis

A small, privately held company, Jetage Corporation, is being considered for purchase by a publicly held firm. After the purchase offer has been accepted and while due diligence is being conducted to assess the company's potential, Jetage's revenues begin to fall short of projections. The founder, George Englund, wants to control the information being shared by his chief financial officer, Joe Howard. Can Joe comply with his boss's request even if he questions whether it is the right thing to do?

Detailed Narrative

Joe Howard had been hired as chief financial officer of Jetage Corporation, a rapidly growing privately held company. Within two years, it had become nationally recognized, with annual revenues of just under $100 million. With the value and success of the company, its founder, George Englund, decided to sell to a larger publicly traded corporation. The timing for selling seemed optimal to obtain the maximum value for the company.

When one company makes an offer to purchase another, there is an investigative process known as due diligence, to enable the buyer to make an informed decision about the purchase. Generally speaking, the seller is motivated to maximize the sale price, whereas the buyer wants to pay as little as possible. The due diligence process provides the buyer an opportunity to uncover any problems and potentially negotiate a lower sale price. The due diligence process may become somewhat adversarial, as seller and buyer can be at odds with each other.

During the due diligence process, Jetage Corporation fell short of projected revenue expectations. Thus, the buyer raised concerns and requested updated financial projections to ensure it was making a sound investment. Receiving this request, Englund met with his key executives to make sure that only information he approved would be given to the buyer.

When meeting with Joe Howard, Englund said that he wanted financial projections prepared that would enable him to get the initial sales price. He read out loud a particular section from the sales contract that stated the buyer should place no reliance on any projected financial data provided by Jetage. This contractual language was to protect it from future litigation by placing responsibility on the buyer to verify the information received through the due diligence process. After Englund delivered his message, there was no discussion about alternative courses of action or potential consequences, and the meeting ended.

Joe walked away from the meeting wondering how he had gotten into such a mess. If he did not comply with the founder's request to prepare the forecast accordingly, he risked losing his job immediately. He also was putting his career in jeopardy should the owner start to badmouth him in the business community. But if he did comply with the request, Joe felt he would be aiding the owner in defrauding the buyer and its stakeholders. What should he do?

Additional Questions to Consider

1. Consequences: What are the potential consequences for each of the stakeholders involved if the CFO were to comply with the founder's request?

2. Professional standards: As a member of the Association for Accountants and Financial Professionals in Business as well as the American Institute of CPAs, Joe has professional standards of conduct and ethics to direct his practice. How do these professional standards and his obligations as a member differ from his obligations to Jetage Corporation and its founder?

3. Moral imagination: Considering the desires and duties of all stakeholders, what options might be considered and/or rehearsed if you were the CFO?

4. Social order conflicts: To what extent does the hierarchical relationship between the company founder and its CFO need to be considered? How do you factor this into your consideration of what is good and right in this case?

5. Errors of omission: What responsibility does a CFO have to alert a potential buyer about these kinds of financial concerns? Given that the buyer is a publicly held corporation with a number of shareholders, if its due diligence committee assumes (incorrectly) that it is receiving accurate reports, could Joe suggest to the committee that it look deeper or talk with other people? Or should Joe remain outside the due diligence circle or offer to help with the process?

Case 2: Family Obligations

Synopsis

Bob's only sibling, Karen, is homeless again. In the past he has given her money and sought social services to address her various human service needs. Now at middle age, Karen is becoming increasingly unable to control her life. She's called upon her brother for help to get sober. Should Bob sacrifice some of his own dreams to provide resources for her?

Detailed Narrative

Bob and Karen grew up in a middle-class family where Dad was the traditional breadwinner and Mom stayed at home. The neighborhood was full of other children their ages with whom to play. Older brother Bob always took care of his little sister and made sure she was safe. All in all, life for the family appeared to be fairly normal.

But entering adolescence, the siblings took different paths. Bob focused on school to fulfill his dream of becoming a social worker to help his community. Karen didn't really care about school and prioritized partying with friends. As a young adult, her life was marked by failed relationships, drug addiction, and bouts of homelessness. She moved to a different part of the country and was heard from sporadically, usually when she needed money. There would be occasional encounters with the law that led to her being admitted to detox and raising hopes for redemption. Unfortunately she always returned to the street life that she knew.

Bob, in the meantime, graduated from college, secured a social work job and returned to his hometown to care for his parents as they aged. It was heartbreaking to watch their hopes for Karen be rekindled, only to have them dashed. Not knowing where she was or how to contact her caused deep pain for their parents, who watched Karen live a life neither of them ever imagined for her.

Now that his parents were gone and he had no spouse or children of his own, Karen was his only family. Bob considered encouraging her to come back home to live with him, getting away from the life and habits she had, but he also knew how deep her addictions were. The likelihood of her bringing drugs into his home was great, and he feared his livelihood would be at stake if she came to live with him. He wondered "At what point is there an ethical right to protect one's own interests?" It frustrated and hurt him that she called only when she needed something.

Out of the blue, Karen called asking for his support to enter a drug treatment facility. She sounded more remorseful than ever before, declaring her resolution to do better in her life. She counted on his love, support, and financial assistance to break her drug addiction.

Bob was reflective about this prospect especially in light of the number of times she had repeated this pattern. But the treatment program was stellar, and he knew of its reputation for "saving the drowning" addicts. It was also expensive. Nearing retirement, he realized things were going to be tight especially if he were to finance Karen's treatment.

What was his responsibility to his sister? What was his responsibility as a Christian man honoring the gospel that said "Whatever you do to the least of these you do unto me?" Was she even able to make the needed changes after spending most of her life addicted and in unstable relationships? Was his sister's potential homelessness a reason to put himself in a highly vulnerable position in his retirement? What were his ethical responsibilities?

Additional Questions to Consider

1. Conflicting duties to self and other: Bob questions "At what point is there an ethical right to protect one's own interests?" Is there a point at which self-sacrifice for another is no longer ethical? When does a duty to self take precedent? To whom should Bob be most responsible?

2. Addiction behavior: How does drug addiction play into this case? Is there a difference in ethical obligation when a person fails to take responsibility for his or her own behavior? What if Karen no longer

has the capacity to make her own decisions? How does this factor into the DIRR process?

3. Religious beliefs: How might Bob's religious values and beliefs as a Christian play into in this case?

4. Family obligations: What are Bob's family obligations to his sister? To what extent does it matter that they are the only surviving members of the family, that he has no family of his own besides his sister?

5. Good outcomes: What good outcomes might be desirable in this case for Bob and for Karen?

Case 3: Broken Trust

Synopsis

Through the use of social media, a youth director discovers a young person in her care engaging in behavior that is risky to himself and others. Does she violate the trust she has established with him and other youth to confront him or to report his behavior to his parents? The negative consequences of exposing his behavior seem huge but so do not reporting his activities.

Detailed Narrative

Jennifer Johnson is in her fourth year as the full-time director of youth services at a large suburban YMCA. At the heart of her leadership is building relationships with young people, providing opportunities for them to develop their talents and leadership.

Attendance at youth events is growing at the Y especially those designed to develop the leadership of young people. There is a mentoring program pairing older students as mentors with younger students, and those selected must vie to become mentors, receiving special training when they are accepted. Parents were happy with the youth services, and Jennifer's annual reviews from her supervisor were glowing. So far, so good!

A young adult herself, Jennifer is in a privileged position, as many young people talk regularly with her about matters that they probably don't discuss at home. She keeps conversations in confidence and is committed to maintaining the students' trust. She often "friends" them on her social media network and is befriended by them as well. This, too, she considers a privilege, as most parents are not given such access.

One January morning when Jennifer logged in to her account, she saw pictures of Harrison, one of her youth leaders and a mentor to younger students. He is a talented young man with much to offer as a leader in the program. However, the pictures she saw on the website displayed a young person participating in underage drinking and possibly smoking pot at a friend's party.

One weekend after seeing the pictures and reading the social media postings, Jennifer realized that Harrison was no longer endangering just himself, as he often drove his friends to and from events. What about Harrison's role as a mentor to younger people who might also see the pictures? Had he become a liability to others in the program? Suddenly she felt that she could not ignore it or hope for the best. She had to do something, but what? If confronted, could he simply remove her name from the social network site or deny that anything was wrong?

Rehearsing her options she had to consider whether she would stop there. What if something tragic were to happen, and her boss or his parents came to her to ask whether she knew of his inappropriate social behavior? Did she have a responsibility to share what she knew? How might the other students react? Would they still trust her?

Could she lose her job if the YMCA were to find out that she knew he was in trouble and didn't do anything? Were the relationships with the students and the trust they had in her more important than job security? Fifteen percent of the funding for the Y was from the state government to provide these programs, which requires the Y staff to comply with all mandatory notification laws. Were there other key players she needed to consider? There seemed to be more at stake than she initially realized.

Additional Questions to Consider

1. Democracy: Balancing the needs of the one with the needs of the group is at the heart of Dewey's concept of democracy. How would you sort this out if you were Jennifer?
2. Duty versus duty: Jennifer has a duty to her employer (and the parents) as well as a duty to youth whom she mentors. How would you articulate the content of these duties? What would you include in rehearsing a way to address all of these duties?
3. Private versus public interests: Is this a private matter with the young man, or does it have consequences for the youth organization as a whole? How does the fact that he plays a leadership role in the youth program enter into this case?
4. Key players: As Jennifer identifies the key players in this situation, do you agree with her inclusion of herself, the young man, his parents, the supervisor, and the other youth? What options do you suggest for the rehearsal that takes all of these stakeholders into account? What moral action would you take if you were Jennifer?
5. Employer's perspective: What expectations do you have of your employees who oversee or care for others, especially minors? Does the kind of organization make a difference in these expectations? If so, how?

Case 4: Honoring the Blue Line

Synopsis

Brad Ng, a rookie police officer, is completing his field training under an experienced field training officer (FTO) John Valdez. In response to a domestic case, the FTO screams and kicks the abuser. His write-up of the incident does not document those actions. John expects Brad as the rookie to sign off on the case. Will the rookie "rat out" his superior officer for inappropriate and unnecessary use of force, or will Brad honor the "blue line" to become one of them?

Detailed Narrative

Brad Ng's dream of becoming a police officer had finally come true. After working for three years as a community service officer, he had been hired by the city to become a licensed police officer. He completed the six weeks of police academy training on various aspects of policing—use of weapons, constitutional law, discretionary powers, and interviewing techniques. Part of the training included a lecture on ethics and the expectations held by both the community and the department.

In the next phase of his training, Brad was assigned to a field training officer (FTO), who would help the rookie transition from the classroom to the beat, establishing protocols, teaching practical responses, and making split-second decisions on the job. As the final aspect of police training, the FTO has the power to fail a rookie by communicating to the superiors that the rookie does not have what it takes to be a successful police officer. The awareness of this power of the FTO haunts many rookies and became the source of Brad's dilemma. John Valdez, his FTO, made a point of telling him daily, "You may have learned XYZ in the academy, but this is the way things are really done around here."

Spending hours together each day, the experienced officer could question Brad and assess his knowledge and skills. At times John pushed the rookie to take actions that Brad specifically mentioned as something he dreaded. About the third time it happened, Brad realized he was being tested. Was he willing to obey John's orders despite his own ethical concerns about the situation?

Overall, the experiences on the street had been incredible. Brad learned to respect John's knowledge of the community and his commitment to making good officers from rookies. He learned about John's background and that he had no tolerance for domestic abusers, as his sister had suffered greatly at the hands of her former husband.

One night a domestic abuse call came in for their response. Officer Valdez took the lead on this one and within minutes had the suspect subdued on the ground. Screaming at the suspect, he began kicking him repeatedly. Brad saw this as a potential case of police brutality, for the suspect had already submitted to the officer's orders and was on the ground in handcuffs.

After taking the suspect to jail, John told Brad, "I will write this incident up and you sign it and turn it in." The report that came to Brad to sign and submit noted how the suspect had fought with John, a fight that continued once he was on the ground, resulting in probable injuries to the suspect.

Brad knew that was not what happened, and he also knew that his potential career as a police officer was on the line. If he were caught lying, it would essentially end his career, as any lawyer could bring it forth as evidence to reduce his credibility on the witness stand. If he refused to sign, John would likely accuse him of not "honoring the blue line." He could report that the rookie did not have what it would take to be a successful officer, and Brad would simply be let go by the department. If the rookie decided to report the deception to his superiors, John might deny it and Brad might be reputed to be a "snitch."

The document was still on his desk at the end of his shift. What should the rookie officer do?

Additional Questions to Consider

1. Power differential: As FTO, John has greater power over the rookie, and this leaves Brad feeling vulnerable. How do you account for the power differences in considering Brad's decision?
2. Disregard of policy: In this situation John uses force on a suspect by repeatedly kicking an already handcuffed individual. What are the potential consequences of his actions?
3. Conflicting ethics: How would you describe Brad's conflicting duties and desires? How might you choose between these ethical tensions?
4. Stakeholders: Initially Brad sees this as an ethical conflict with John. Are other stakeholders involved? If so, who might they be? Once they are considered, how does it impact your thinking about this case?

Case 5: Caring for a Minor

Synopsis

A registered nurse, Terry manages the caseload of a highly regarded orthopedic surgeon who specializes in complex spinal surgeries. She is currently working with a young client who needs surgery to halt the progression of her scoliosis. But the patient's parents do not give consent for the operation even though the patient wants it. Issues of culture increase the complexity of the situation.

Detailed Narrative

Kia is a 14-year-old, second-generation Hmong who has been diagnosed with scoliosis. The curve in her spine is worsening and not responding to the bracing treatment. As a result, the orthopedic surgeon is recommending fusing Kia's spine to prevent further debilitation. A complicated surgery, the results have been promising though not guaranteed. Timing of the surgery is critical, as her back will continue to curve, Younger patients are better candidates for successful intervention, but it does mean that Kia will be in a cast and require significant care in the weeks following surgery.

For Terry, as nurse manager of the case, the ethics of Kia's situation are haunting and complex. As the disease progresses, the body curves in on itself, with serious impacts on the lungs, gastrointestinal system, and mobility and balance, and the pain associated with these issues increases. Terry knows that the earlier it can be corrected the fewer the long-term problems would be for Kia. But Terry is also aware that the surgery is not a guarantee and Kia might still be in pain.

When she answered the questions posed by Kia and reiterated the options, the girl made it clear that she wants to have the surgery now. She does not want to wait until she is 18, when she could have the surgery without her parent's consent. She wants the best possible outcome and is afraid that waiting four more years will have negative consequences.

Talking with Kia's parents, Terry felt that they were not receptive. Although they desired a better and less painful life for their child, they did not agree with the proposed surgery. There were a number of factors that entered into their decision.

First, they were already skeptical of the medical proposals made by the doctors and nurses. Many in their community distrusted Western medicine, preferring their own Asian approaches to healing the body.

Second, the traditional Hmong belief was that cutting into the body may allow bad spirits to enter. For Kia's parents, to consent to the surgery could have disastrous spiritual consequences for their daughter.

Third, that their daughter would defy the family's wishes seemed unthinkable. The father should be making such an important decision on his daughter's behalf, not the child. How could he face the community if that happened?

Terry felt a great deal of tension as she faced the reality of the disagreement between Kia and her parents. Her own personal and professional values favored the surgery, but she wondered "Had the risks and options been adequately explained in a way that Kia's parents could understand since they were not native English speakers?" The interpreter might not have presented the medical information sufficiently to the parents.

Could the staff develop a treatment plan that would honor the values and beliefs of Kia and her family as well as the professional obligations to provide her the best treatment? When does a failure to act constitute medical neglect? What is the responsibility of the health care team when a family cannot agree on a treatment plan?

The team did want to maintain trust with the family in order to monitor Kia's condition and provide appropriate noninvasive treatments as her scoliosis progresses. Terry wondered whether the Hmong community recognizes the risks that Kia faces by not having surgery. On the other hand, as a member of the majority culture and medical community, Terry wondered whether her biases devalued the family decision on behalf of their minor child.

The hospital's standard operating procedure is that whenever possible they will delay surgery until everyone agrees. What if that doesn't happen? How might they get there? How could Terry support Kia as well as the family in this decision?

Additional Questions to Consider

1. Defining the good: How does the "good" in this situation change if the treatment plan threatens the relationship between the parents and the child or between the family and their community, or causes a disagreement between the parents?

2. Honoring another's culture: Terry has to be intentional about accounting for very different understandings about what it means to have surgery. From her perspective as a medical professional, the operation was a life-altering way to address Kia's scoliosis, but her family does not agree. How might the DIRR process help work through these differences?

3. Acknowledging information gaps: Judgments are made based on what people know (and don't know). In a dilemma like this with multiple parties coming from very different perspectives, how would you provide the necessary information for everyone involved?

4. Individual versus group: In your profession, what does it take to move beyond what is best for one individual to recognize the values and culture of the people involved?

5. Rehearsing the options: How might Terry get everyone to agree? How would you rediscern this situation with that goal in mind?

Case 6: Middle Management

Synopsis

As a newly hired director of a government office, Jessica learns that the organizational values and mission are not being practiced as she had thought. She finds herself caught between those she supervises and those to whom she reports. Is she merely a messenger shuffling back and forth? At the end of her first year, should she stay on even though she feels these ethical tensions?

Detailed Narrative

Settling into a new position as a director in a government agency, Jessica was excited to be working at a place that valued its employees and encouraged their engagement in decision making. The agency's mission fit well with Jessica's participatory leadership style and ways of working with people, or so she thought.

But listening to the managers who reported to her, she learned of their anger and frustration over the ways things had been working. There was little communication from the top and even less regard for grassroots input. She recognized and valued the loyalty and insights of these long-term government employees. What they shared about the work, as well as their caring for one another, was truly amazing. She wanted to make sure upper level administration recognized this work too.

Unfortunately, it appeared that the current administration really was not interested in engaging the staff; rather, they wanted the middle managers like Jessica to communicate and implement the changes that the policy makers had made, not question them or raise concerns. No one seemed to listen to the ideas, suggestions, and honest scrutiny she brought up from her unit. Even the person who had hired her had moved on to a different position, resulting in a new supervisor.

Feeling alone and unsupported at the end of her first year Jessica went to the person who had hired her to discuss her options, specifically how to negotiate a return to her former position. She had return rights if she wanted to go back. He urged her to stay, saying that her supervisors thought she was doing a great job and it was too soon to quit. Jessica was uneasy, knowing she would have not taken this job if she'd known how little they valued their employees despite what their mission and values stated. If she were to stay, how could she work the situation to negotiate the ethical tensions she experienced between her own values, the values of her supervisees, and the habits and values of those above her?

Additional Questions to Consider

1. The ethics of change: Organizations spend much time and money orienting new employees. Besides training for basic tasks and compensation for work done, what duties do organizations have toward their employees? Could a new middle-level manager institute change under the radar?

2. The hiring process: How would you describe the mission and values of an organization to a candidate in the midst of a hiring process? What are the respective duties and desires of the organization and its employees? What could these parties have done differently to find a better fit between employee and organization? How might social justice ethics impact a hiring process?

3. The milieu of middle managers: Jessica found herself in the middle of two very difficult cultures—a participatory team that grew in trust and honesty under her leadership and an executive team with a clear hierarchy that expected her to do what she was told. She also found herself caught between valuing the stated mission and vision of the organization and executive leaders who did not. Rehearse options for Jessica for each of these tensions.

SUMMARY

Six additional cases were presented in this chapter for the reader's consideration. Each case included a synopsis, a detailed narrative, and some discussion questions. As in the previous chapter, the cases present problems and suggest ethical tensions that result from incidents and/or situations that challenge the decision maker. The reader is invited to explore the contexts, consider the key players, propose alternatives, and rehearse resolutions. Discussing how to work through the ethical tensions toward resolution takes practice. We hope these cases give you the opportunity to do that.

TEN

Teaching Ethical Deliberation

Ten years ago when we began this book project, our motivation was to write something that would provide our students the necessary foundation and method for grappling with the ethical dilemmas in their professional lives. We wanted to provide sufficient background for them to understand the complexity of ethical problems, consider how tensions arise from different ways of reasoning, and negotiate among many divergent viewpoints.

Our assumptions were grounded in the need for democratic leadership, taking into account differences among individuals while at the same time seeking to emphasize the common goals and aspirations that draw us together as a society. We proposed the DIRR inquiry method, based in democratic ethics and applied as an overarching framework for thinking through messy leadership problems and situations.

Back then Bruce was the department chairperson of an educational leadership program for preparing school administrators. He taught an ethics course that served as a capstone in the licensure programs at St. Thomas. Ernestine was a faculty member teaching ethics for aspiring school leaders at the University of Hawaii. For both, the focus of this book was toward supporting the ethical development of school leaders.

Today we are in different places. Bruce became dean of his college, taking it through national accreditation and adjusting to increasing business pressures in higher education. While he continued to teach ethics at the doctoral level, he did less with the educational leadership program that he had chaired. Still a faculty member, Ernestine has taught less in the field of ethics than previously. There have been greater demands placed on her to teach core courses rather than electives such as ethical decision making.

149

In concluding this second edition, we reflect upon our paths over these intervening years, comparing and contrasting approaches and contexts. Some reflections relate to our teaching and the pedagogy employed in class to foster ethical deliberation and leadership. We also comment on the changes in our own lives beyond the classroom that have influenced our teaching of educational and other leaders to employ democratic practices. We conclude with some thoughts about more general applications for ethical decision making and leadership.

TEACHING NARRATIVES

We teach at different institutions (a private parochial institution and a public research-extensive university) in the Midwest and Pacific. We have chosen to write separate narratives to describe the ethics courses taught as situated within our differently configured leadership preparation programs.

Written in the first person, our individual narratives present how we choose to teach about ethics and ethical deliberation. We note specific institutional contexts and teaching challenges that have influenced us, offering contrasts of how we have approached the teaching of leadership ethics, but more importantly, how we have encouraged our students to create their own ethical spaces.

Bruce Kramer—University of St. Thomas, Minneapolis

A diocesan Catholic institution of higher education, the University of St. Thomas is situated in downtown Minneapolis. The context of teaching here includes social, cultural, economic, and historical tensions arising from the university's beginnings as a small liberal arts Catholic college for men. Since then, it has evolved to include professional schools of business, law, and social work, as well as education and psychology. Inevitably there are tensions between having a Catholic mission and preparing students for the secular world of public leadership.

In 2006, I took on service in the central administration of my college, appointed first as associate dean, then interim dean, and later dean, serving until 2012. Throughout my deanship, I continued to teach the doctoral course in ethics. In addition, I represented college administrators on the Minnesota Board of School Administrators and served on the board's ethics committee, where all ethical complaints about licensed administrators statewide were examined. These varied experiences gave me a much broader view of working ethical situations, as I found myself not only teaching but living the ethical dilemmas discussed in the courses I taught. I felt that the board work brought me a much more urgent view to the ethical methodology proposed in this book.

The doctoral course I taught, "Leadership Ethics," is a core require-ment in our program. Its focus is to ensure that St. Thomas doctoral students see the moral language in their own leadership situations and can identify actions for themselves that are ethically compatible with their own beliefs and values. I shared this teaching with my colleague Dr. Deb DeMeester, and together we established the following outcomes:

Students are to develop sharpened understanding of

- ethical history and philosophy,
- the student's own moral leadership capacity,
- the areas of possible conflict between their values and those of oth-ers, and
- the consequences of conscious and unconscious ethical decisions by both the student and others.

They would be able to

- analyze the ethical dimensions of a situation,
- communicate an understanding of the ethical dimensions of any dilemma,
- seek ethical solutions to problems that look unsolvable, and
- imagine moral outcomes in situations for which moral solutions are not immediately discernible.

They develop a heightened appreciation of

- an ethical inquiry method;
- the underlying ethical considerations of a personal/professional di-lemma;
- the ethical questions raised by privilege, difference, and cultural traditions;
- the forces shaping a student's own ethical beliefs; and
- the ethical connection and interdependence between desired self and the world desired.

The students in the doctoral course represent varied professions—K–12 educator; school administrator; business entrepreneur; engineer; non-profit manager; and public safety, police, and fire administration person-nel. This variety of occupations and interests enables the class to have rich discussions about the nature of ethics, leadership opportunities, and challenges in different contexts, making for broader learning experiences for all of us.

The single most important assignment in the course is an iterative paper detailing a difficult ethical problem, either personal or profession-al, that our students will work using the DIRR method. This has led us to explore situations that we might never have imagined, including personal family decisions around illness, death, and dying as well as complex institutional issues that challenge students' personal moral beliefs.

The DIRR method surfaces a myriad of implications for the individual student. Although the cases are kept confidential between student and instructor, on the last day of the course we ask the students to give a brief presentation. These are not about their cases in particular but about what they have learned about themselves utilizing an ethical deliberative process.

Given the tremendous time spent on course readings, class discussions, personal reflection, and writing, the students have responded enthusiastically. For example, one student commented,

> This class has challenged me to move outside of my analytic comfort zone and challenge where the line of demarcation lies between what is "right" versus what is "wrong" and what is "good" versus what is "bad."

Another student spoke of a personal awareness that evolved for her:

> This course has contributed not only to my personal discernment over dilemmas at home and at work, but has also helped me to define me. Me the mother, me the wife, me the friend, me the leader, me the individual . . . me the child of God.

While ten years of co-teaching with Deb DeMeester has led to a closeness whereby we would often complete each other's sentences, our collaborative partnership was seriously tested two years ago by a change in life circumstances. In December 2010, two months before the beginning of the 2011 spring semester, I was diagnosed with amyotrophic lateral sclerosis (ALS), a disease of the nerve cells in the brain and spinal cord controlling all voluntary muscle movement. ALS is also known as Lou Gehrig's disease. The feelings and the sense of loss associated with such a terminal diagnosis were indescribable.

At the time, I knew that I would need to modify how I engaged with both teaching and leading the college. With Deb's wholehearted support and encouragement, I continued teaching albeit in a less fully engaged capacity. I was very lucky that she could pick up many responsibilities that I could no longer physically fulfill. And we successfully made it through two semesters!

Needless to say, my teaching has undergone significant evolution, forged by the forces of higher education leadership, Minnesota Board service, and terminal disease. Earlier in my teaching career, I saw my role more as provocateur in order to challenge students' thinking and decision making. With this type of teaching style, I aimed to push and prod my sometimes complacent students into seeing differently and acting boldly. However, I found provocation to be less satisfying as process and less useful in terms of outcomes. I felt I was intellectually shifting my frame of reference in how I was teaching, and it took the diagnosis of ALS to truly solidify that change.

For me, this book had been about an applied inquiry method that I thought might result in better leadership preparation for my students. ALS has enhanced my own ability to encompass the complex world presented in the lives of these remarkable human beings beyond any capability I ever thought possible. The overarching ethic of my life began to parallel that of this book—democratic leadership, empirical knowledge, moral creativity—all informed by a life fully engaged by the disease ALS.

I feel a deepened love for both students and colleagues that transcends the professional boundaries erected in the name of educational leadership. I learned over the past two years that the most powerful and transformative morality begins in love. I would argue that the toughest cases, the most bitter and mean-spirited leadership situations, are nothing more than a disengagement of this most human of gifts. Our academic concepts take on new meaning when seen through a lens of love for each other. We are granted very little time, and each of us will face death one day. Why not seek meaningful human engagement in the process? Why not seek the respect and esteem implied in democracy?

So my teaching has changed, first informed by a leadership position that applied ethical theory from day one, and then refined by the most human condition of facing my own mortality accelerated before its time. And I believe that has led to a sense of urgency to be engaging in a way that is deeply spiritual, lovingly kind, and profoundly ethical.

Ernestine Enomoto—University of Hawaii, Manoa, Honolulu

Since 1998, I have taught at the University of Hawaii, Manoa, a research-extensive university in the state of Hawaii. It is Hawaii's flagship institution, serving statewide needs for undergraduate and graduate education in all disciplines. Our College of Education provides the majority of the teacher educators, special educators, and school administrators for the unified state system of education.

In our Educational Administration Department, we offer a seminar in ethics as a special topics offering. That is, the same course number, EDEA780, may refer to a course on different topics such as curriculum issues, professional socialization, and adult learning styles, as well as ethics. Currently there is no specifically designated course on the study of ethics in our program. The ethics seminar is an elective for those interested in the topic or with a need to fulfill the one-seminar requirement in their administrative preparation.

In the past, faculty members have taught ethics from a philosophical perspective and have emphasized historical and theoretical aspects of study, with limited connections made to any practical application of ethics. Building upon ethical deliberation as well as understanding ethical reasoning, I developed my course emphasizing the importance of ethical decision making for effective educational leaders.

In the course, I propose that school administrators need to know how to learn, adapt, and make on-the-spot decisions based on qualities of value and character. Accordingly they must be able to reflect upon their own individual values and beliefs in education as well as their understanding of the community in which they live. My course offers students a journey of inquiry and exploration in the ways we think through ethical dilemmas and make decisions as school leaders.

The course begins by having students articulate a personal vision and values. They think through what they deem most important about education and their role as educators and leaders. They also collaboratively construct a viable vision for the whole class, as all students share what they view as most important for our learning environment and determine priorities collectively. This shared vision becomes our framework for class discussions and participation throughout the term.

Using both the personal and shared vision statements, students examine various reality-based educational scenarios with issues such as conflict of interest, equal opportunity, confidentiality, and individual rights and responsibilities. Given the DIRR method, students are asked to determine whether the scenario poses an ethical dilemma and, if so, to apply at least three principles of ethical reasoning.

For example, they might contrast the duty-based ethics with desires-based ethics, identifying the rationale and arguments for each case. They might consider what other ethical tensions might factor into deciding what to do. Could one's personal virtues be called into question to make sound judgments? Do social order issues related to power and authority confound one's decision making? If so, how?

Students engage privately in writing about the cases as well as discussing them in small groups or with the whole class. These simulated situations provide realistic and often relevant scenarios to their life experiences. Class discussions include time for students to present varying viewpoints. In some cases, we "try on each other's shoes" to examine alternative perspectives and consider consequences from diverse viewpoints. We try on a position different from our personal preference to understand that point of view better. Students usually work through the logic and argument in small groups before presenting their position to the class.

Throughout the term, they compile a portfolio of four different cases, with each write-up describing an ethical dilemma and providing supporting rationale, evidence gathered, and appropriate references. At least one case must be an original, meaning that they come up with the example themselves. This offers an opportunity to think of how to be objective given their own positionality and biases in the case.

As the teacher, I give feedback along the way and encourage students to revise their write-ups throughout the term. Often they choose to re-write their first cases as their understanding and reasoning develop throughout the course.

Finally, students reflect upon the entire portfolio and prepare a summative statement about it. This overall reflection gives them a chance to identify ethical considerations in their individual administrative decision making and to develop personal and professional guidelines for making such decisions.

After taking the course, students have commented on increasing their ability to problem solve, work through the ethical issues involved, and think through challenging questions relevant to their lives. In the words of one student, the course "helped tremendously in developing and sharpening our decision-making capabilities." Another said,

> I have come to realize the importance of really putting yourself in another's place, examining an issue from multiple angles, practicing ethical decision making, and being a facilitative leader.

One former student came up to me several years after finishing the program and recalled our ethics course. "It was the best course in my ed admin program."

COMPARING TEACHING APPROACHES

Reflecting upon our teaching, we identified our similarities and differences. First, in terms of similarities, we strive to include diverse viewpoints through our selected readings and discussions. We offer contrasting and often critical perspectives in the readings for the course. Bruce and Deb draw upon the critical theorists to probe what might be taken for granted. Varied multiple perspectives are encouraged through lively class discussions, debate, and dialogue.

A second similarity in our teaching approaches is that we encourage our students to clarify their own codes of ethics. Ernestine has students write out their personal codes and apply them in making decisions. Bruce and Deb invite their students to refine their viewpoints as they write their cases. We feel that this type of values clarification helps students work through the process of translating their thinking into personal and professional values that inform ethical actions as demonstrated in their writing.

A third similarity is that, like Shapiro and Stefkovich (2005) and Strike, Haller, and Soltis (1998), we employ case narratives in considering how to make ethical decisions. Examples of these are found in the book. But students are encouraged to write their own narratives and describe situations using ethical language. Utilizing the DIRR method, we expect that students will demonstrate thoughtful introspection and critical reflection as they deliberate on what to do and what will result.

Our teaching approaches are also different in part because of our contexts. Teaching at a parochial institution, Bruce and Deb have doctoral students in a cohort, who are primarily but not exclusively in education. By contrast, Ernestine teaches mostly master's students in educational administration in a public university setting. Such differences lead to different styles of teaching in ensuring that a variety of perspectives are presented. For example, to encourage students to probe their own views, Ernestine has them act out roles in small groups whereby they have to defend a viewpoint that they might not necessarily agree with. This dramatic enactment provides for an opportunity to walk in another's shoes.

As stated above, we both try to support our students in clarifying their individual ethical codes. This is a point of convergence for us. We carry a strong value for individual students in our classrooms. We honor every student's slightly different approach and strive to allow for their individual differences as they explore their own personal beliefs. We agree that through the clarification of their belief systems, particularly as they compare their beliefs with their espoused sense of actions, they attain meaningful learning.

CHALLENGES IN TEACHING

Our teaching challenges can be characterized in terms of the continuum of the contexts in which we teach. We agree that where and whom we teach are important factors in helping us decide what actions we will take, and the actions taken are not prescribed but rather based on individual diagnosis. We try to exercise the same ethical clarification, reflection, and discernment as our students in determining our own actions. Our actions are part of a continuum, as well, within our respective departments, institutions, field of educational leadership, and current context of standards and accountability in American education.

The standards and accountability movement is a major factor in discussions about American education, whether we are in Hawaii or Minnesota. Ironically, at a time when we are more attentive to individual student needs, legislation directed toward accountability has taken a one-size-fits-all approach, holding everyone to the same academic standards, whether appropriate or not.

We fear that accountability reform means that what is interpreted as ethical behavior for the school leader is increasingly prescribed by the dictates of standards-based education and other accountability factors. It is possible that standards lend themselves to "button-down" thinking about what is right versus wrong. This current context poses the same ethical dilemma in leadership preparation programs as in public education, namely, how to honor individual differences while achieving academic standards directed toward the common good.

Despite concern over external standards, accountability, demands on leadership, and other challenges in teaching, we remain optimistic. If in applying the standards there is the space for inquiry and critique, then we believe it is also possible to encourage critical and original thinking whereby individuals are asked to reflect, discern, and reason through their actions. We have come to identify this as an ethical space that might be present in our teaching of ethical leadership.

ETHICAL SPACE

Recall Dewey's admonition that democracy is the place where the group's responsibility is to maximize the potential of each of its individuals, and the individual's responsibility is to support the group in this process. From this understanding, we look for indicators in our teaching and leadership for whether ethical space is present.

One indicator is the respect for diversity present in the group. To what extent are students' individual perceptions, experiences, values, and beliefs encouraged and shared? Is there an ease of communication within and between different individuals, groups, and social networks? Is there as much listening as there is talking?

A second indicator is the level of trust and openness that is present in the classroom. Do individuals feel open to each other's viewpoints? Can everyone share freely and honestly? Has trust developed among the individuals over time? How might we allow our own views to be challenged by other perspectives and experiences?

A third indicator of the presence of an ethical space is the opportunity to employ methods both critical and analytical. We offer the DIRR method to push beyond the collective sharing and "feel good" conversations in attempting problem solving and ethical deliberation. These aims are directed toward a collective good that makes for individual and social growth and development.

A fourth indicator is the commitment of all to participate fully. As teachers, we might set the agenda and establish some of the ground rules, but we need everyone to work collaboratively for this to truly be an ethical space for all. This active engagement underscores the building of democratic ethics whereby there is group as well as individual responsibility. This translates directly into engaged citizenry as students' ideas about democratic participation in society.

In our own development as faculty members, academics, and leaders, we have invested in creating such an ethical space. It is no easy task, for it requires ethics to be front and center in any manifestation of leadership. Yet we believe that fostering democratic ethics is the only way to keep us above the juggernaut of institutional hubris and arrogance. We recognize the limitations of our own leadership thinking and attempt to learn from mistakes as well as successes.

TEACHING AND MODELING DEMOCRATIC LEADERSHIP

We want to underscore our belief that prospective and practicing educational leaders need to teach and model democratic leadership in their school communities. In earlier chapters, we discussed how the DIRR method could build the democratic moral capacity of a school over time. But school leaders need to take responsibility for helping others understand and apply the method. This means that time must be spent in establishing the rules and boundaries that the DIRR method of inquiry requires. The leader must learn to put aside ego and model the listening that goes into all good communication. There also needs to be conscious cultural shaping that reinforces the ethical deliberation of teachers, parents, and other participants in the process.

In essence, we are advocating the need to teach and model democratic leadership, not by telling others what to do, but by modeling and facilitating the method. More than ever, we see that school leaders need to actively listen to and honor varied perspectives. Leaders need to be able to negotiate individual differences toward common goals and objectives that benefit the school community.

Rather than being the only leader, they can develop leadership by encouraging the involvement and participation of school or other institutional members. These include those in the wider community as well as those members affiliated directly with the school. We tend not to train leaders this way. Our popular culture still admires the solo heroic leader, and the narratives of effective leadership that are most available to us identify these representations. But there are other models of leadership that foster caring, compassion, and inclusion, starting from within the educational setting and extending into the community at large.

CONCLUDING THOUGHTS

Our focus in this concluding chapter was on the "how" and "where" of teaching ethics. We presented our own teaching approaches but also suggested that ethical deliberation needs to be considered in other venues. Applied ethics can be integrated in classroom teaching through collaboration and shared decision making. We extended this to the role of school administrator and specified how democratic ethics is viable as a framework for a different kind of leadership.

We find ourselves asking whether, during the current context of standards and accountability, there is room for what Heslep (1997) called a philosophical model of leadership with inquiry and philosophical values at the core of leadership decision making. Accountability is about making decisions that produce right actions and good outcomes. As all decisions have ethical implications, the study of ethics and ethical deliberation is central to the ability to truly reform education. We hope the foundations, methods, and applications provided in this book serve to encourage your understanding of the subject. May you find a way to frame your own leadership to produce truly meaningful change in educating our children.

References

Apple, M. W., & Weis, L. (Eds.). (1983). *Ideology and practice in schooling.* Philadelphia, PA: Temple University.

Armstrong, K. (2001). *Buddha.* New York, NY: Penguin.

Athenassoulis, N. (2004). Virtue ethics. In *The Internet Encyclopedia of Philosophy.* Retrieved from www.iep.utm.edu/v/virtue.htm#SH2a.

Augustine, Saint. (1963). *Confessions* (R. Warner, Trans.). New York, NY: Mentor-Omega.

Badaracco, J. L., Jr. (2006). *Questions of character: Illuminating the heart of leadership through literature.* Boston, MA: Harvard Business School.

Beck, L. (1994). *Reclaiming educational administration as a caring profession.* New York, NY: Teachers College, Columbia University.

Beck, L., & Murphy, J. (1994). *Ethics in educational leadership programs: An expanding role.* Thousand Oaks, CA: Corwin.

Belenky, M. F., Clinchy, B. M., Goldberger, N. R., & Tarule, J. M. (1986). *Women's ways of knowing: Development of self, voice, and mind.* New York, NY: Basic Books.

Bellah, R. N., Madsen, R., Sullivan, W. M., Swidler, A., & Tipton, S. M. (1985). *Habits of the heart: Individualism and commitment in American life.* Berkeley, CA: University of California.

Bellah, R. N., Madsen, R., Sullivan, W. M., Swidler, A., & Tipton, S. (1991). *The good society.* New York, NY: Alfred A. Knopf.

Bilimoria, P. (1991). Indian ethics. In P. Singer (Ed.), *A companion to ethics* (pp. 43–57). Malden, MA: Blackwell.

Bogotch, I. E. (2002). Educational leadership and social justice: Practice into theory. *Journal of School Leadership, 12,* 138–156.

Bogtoch, I. E. (2005). *Social justice as an educational construct: Problems and possibilities.* Paper presented at the annual meeting of UCEA, Nashville, Tennessee.

Brown, J. F. (1909). *The American high school.* Norwood, MA: J. S. Cushing/Berwick & Smith.

Brown, K. M. (2004). Leadership for social justice and equity: Weaving a transformative framework and pedagogy. *Educational Administration Quarterly, 40*(1), 79–110.

Bryk, A. S., Bender Sebring, P., Allensworth, E., Luppescu, S., & Easton, J. Q. (2010). *Organizing schools for improvement: Lessons from Chicago.* Chicago, IL: The University of Chicago.

Buckle, S. (1991). Natural law. In P. Singer (Ed.), *A companion to ethics* (pp. 161–174). Malden, MA: Blackwell.

Cambron-McCabe, N. (2010). Preparation and development of school leaders: Implications for social justice policies. In C. Marshall & M. Oliva (Eds.), *Leadership for social justice: Making revolutions in education* (2nd ed., pp. 35–54). Boston, MA: Allyn & Bacon.

Cambron-McCabe, N., & McCarthy, M. M. (2005). Educating school leaders for social justice. *Educational Policy, 19,* 201–222.

Capper, C. A., & Frattura, E. M. (2008). *Meeting the needs of students of ALL abilities: How leaders go beyond inclusion.* Thousand Oaks, CA: Corwin.

Capper, C. A., Theoharis, G., & Sebastian, J. (2006). Toward a framework for preparing leaders for social justice. *Journal of Educational Administration, 44*(3), 209–224.

Conley, S., & Enomoto, E. K. (2009). Organizational routines in flux: A case study of change in recording and monitoring student attendance. *Education and Urban Society, 41,* 364–386.

Cordeiro, P. A., & Cunningham, W. G. (2013). *Educational leadership: A bridge to improved practice* (5th ed.). Boston, MA: Pearson.

Council of Chief State School Officers. (2001). *ISLLC standards.* Retrieved from www.ccsso.org/standards.html.

Dantley, M. E., & Tillman, L. C. (2010). Social justice and moral transformative leadership. In C. Marshall & M. Oliva (Eds.), *Leadership for social justice: Making revolutions in education* (2nd ed., pp. 19–34). New York, NY: Pearson.

Darling-Hammond, L. (2010). *The flat world and education: How America's commitment to equity will determine our future.* New York, NY: Teachers College, Columbia University.

Darling-Hammond, L., LaPointe, M. M., Meyerson, D., Orr, M. T., & Cohen, C. (2009). *Preparing school leaders for a changing world: Lessons from exemplary leadership development programs.* Palo Alto, CA: Stanford University, Educational Leadership Institute.

Delmar, R. (2001). What Is feminism? In A. C. Herrmann & A. J. Stewart (Eds.), *Theorizing feminism: Parallel trends in the humanities and social sciences* (2nd ed., pp. 5–28). Boulder, CO: Westview.

Dewey, J. (1916). Middle works: Volume 9. Democracy and education. In L. Hickman (Ed.), *The collected works of John Dewey, 1882–1953: Electronic edition.* Carbondale, IL: The Center for Dewey Studies, 1996.

Dewey, J. (1927). Later works: Volume 2. The public and its problems. In L. Hickman (Ed.), *The collected works of John Dewey, 1882–1953: Electronic edition.* Carbondale, IL: The Center for Dewey Studies, 1996.

Dewey, J. (1930). Later works: Volume 5. Essays: Three independent factors in morals. In L. Hickman (Ed.), *The collected works of John Dewey, 1882–1953: Electronic edition.* Carbondale, IL: The Center for Dewey Studies, 1996.

Dewey, J. (1934). *A common faith.* New Haven, CT: Yale University.

Dewey, J. (1938). Later works: Volume 10. Art as experience. In L. Hickman (Ed.), *The collected works of John Dewey, 1882–1953: Electronic edition.* Carbondale, IL: The Center for Dewey Studies, 1996.

Dewey, J., & Tufts, J. (1932a). Later Works: Volume 7. Ethics. In L. Hickman (Ed.), *The collected works of John Dewey, 1882–1953: Electronic edition.* Carbondale, IL: The Center for Dewey Studies, 1996.

Dewey, J., & Tufts, J. H. (1932b). *Moral education* (Rev. ed.). New York, NY: Henry Holt & Sons.

Edmonds, R. (1979). Effective schools for the urban poor. *Educational Leadership, 37,* 15–24.

Enomoto, E. K. (1997). Negotiating the ethics of care and justice. *Educational Administration Quarterly, 33*(3), 351–370.

Fasching, D. J., deChant, D., & Lantigua, D. M. (2011). *Comparative religious ethics: A narrative approach to global ethics* (2nd ed.). Malden, MA: Blackwell.

Feldman, M. S. (2000). Organizational routines as a source of continuous change. *Organization Science, 11*(6), 611–629.

Feldman, S., & Tyson, K. (2007). Preparing school leaders to work for social justice in education. Paper presented at the annual meeting of AERA, Chicago, IL.

Ferguson, K. E. (1984). *The feminist case against bureaucracy.* Philadelphia, PA: Temple University.

Fesmire, S. (2003). *John Dewey and moral imagination.* Bloomington, IN: Indiana University.

Frankena, W. K. (1963). *Ethics.* Englewood Cliffs, NJ: Prentice Hall.

Fullan, M. (2003). *The moral imperative of school leadership.* Thousand Oaks, CA: Corwin.

Fullan, M. G. (1991). *The new meaning of educational change* (2nd ed.). New York, NY: Teachers College, Columbia University.

Furman, G. (2012). Social justice leadership as praxis: Developing capacities through preparation programs. *Educational Administration Quarterly, 48*(2), 191–229.

Garrison, J. W. (1995). *The new scholarship on John Dewey*. The Netherlands: Kluwer Academic Publishers.

Gilligan, C. (1982). *In a different voice: Psychological theory and women's development.* Cambridge, MA: Harvard University.

Giroux, H. A. (1997). *Pedagogy and the politics of hope: Theory, culture and schooling.* Boulder, CO: Westview.

Green, M. (2013, March 14). Senators denounce military rape as victims testify at Capitol Hill hearing. *Daily Beast*. Retrieved from http://www.thedailybeast.com/articles/2013/03/14/senators-denounce-military-rape-as-victims-testify-at-capitol-hill-hearing.html.

Green, R. (1988). *Religion and moral reason*. Oxford, UK: Oxford University.

Greenfield, W. D. (1993). Articulating values and ethics in administrator preparation. In C. Capper (Ed.), *Educational administration in a pluralistic society* (pp. 267–287). Albany, NY: SUNY.

Haddock Seigfried, C. (1999). Socializing democracy: Jane Addams and John Dewey, *Philosophy of the Social Sciences, 29* (2), 207–230 .

Haldane, J. (1991). Medieval and Renaissance ethics. In P. Singer (Ed.), *A companion to ethics* (pp. 133–146). Malden, MA: Blackwell.

Hare-Mustin, R. T., & Marecek, J. (2001). Gender and the meaning of difference: Postmodernism and psychology. In A. C. Herrmann & A. J. Stewart (Eds.), *Theorizing feminism: Parallel trends in the humanities and social sciences* (2nd ed., pp. 78–109). Boulder, CO: Westview.

Hawley, W., & James, R. (2010). Diversity-responsive school leadership. *UCEA Review, 51*(3), 1–5.

Held, V. (1993). *Feminist morality*. Chicago, IL: University of Chicago.

Heslep, R. D. (1997). The practical value of philosophical thought for the ethical dimension of educational leadership. *Educational Administration Quarterly, 33*(1), 67–85.

hooks, b. (1984). *Feminist theory: From margin to center*. Boston, MA: South End.

Houston, B. (1996). Feminism. In J. J. Chambliss (Ed.), *Philosophy of education: An encyclopedia* (pp. 215–220). New York, NY: Garland.

Howley, A., Andrianaivo, S., & Perry, J. (2005). The pain outweighs the gain: Why teachers don't want to become principals. *Teachers College Record, 107*(4), 757–782.

Interstate School Leadership Licensure Consortium (ISLLC). (1996). *Interstate School Leadership Licensure Consortium: Standards for school leaders.* Washington, DC: Council of Chief State School Officers.

Kant, I. (1785). *Introduction to metaphysics of morals*. Retrieved from http://eserver.org/philosophy/kant/intro-to-metaphys-of-morals.txt.

Katz, M. S., Noddings, N., & Strike, K. A. (Eds.). (1999). *Justice and caring: The search for common ground in education*. New York, NY: Teachers College, Columbia University.

Kellner, M. (1991). Jewish ethics. In P. Singer (Ed.), *A companion to ethics* (pp. 82–90). Malden, MA: Blackwell.

Kidder, R. (1995). *How good people make tough choices: Resolving the dilemmas of ethical living*. New York, NY: William Morrow & Company.

Kozol, J. (2005). *The shame of the nation: The restoration of apartheid schooling in America.* New York, NY: Three Rivers.

Kramer, B. H. (2006a). Democracy and democratic ethics. In F. English (Ed.), *The Sage encyclopedia of educational leadership* (Vol. 1). Thousand Oaks, CA: Sage.

Kramer, B. H. (2006b). Ethics. In F. English (Ed.), *The Sage encyclopedia of educational leadership* (Vol. 1). Thousand Oaks, CA: Sage.

Kramer, B. H., Paull, R., & Enomoto, E. K. (2002). Teaching ethics in an era of accountability: Dilemmas and possibilities. Paper presented at the American Educational Research Association, New Orleans, LA.

Kumashiro, K. (2000). Toward a theory of anti-oppressive education. *Review of Educational Research, 70*(1), 25–53.

Kumashiro, K. (2004). *Against common sense.* New York, NY: Routledge Falmer.

Kymlicka, W. (1991). The social contract tradition. In P. Singer (Ed.), *A companion to ethics* (pp. 186–196). Malden, MA: Blackwell.

Lagemann, E. C. (1996). Experimenting with education: John Dewey and Ella Flagg Young at the University of Chicago. *American Journal of Education, 104* (3), 171–185.

LaMagdeleine, D. R., & Kramer, B. H. (1998). Transgression and forgiveness in an international school: A nonmodern case study. *Educational Administration Quarterly, 34*(3), 421–455.

Larson, C. L., & Murtadha, K. (2002) Leadership for social justice. In J. Murphy (Ed.), *The educational leadership challenge: Redefining leadership for the 21st century* (pp. 134–161. Chicago, IL: National Society for the Study of Education.

Levine, A. (2005). *Educating school leaders.* Washington DC: The Education Schools Project.

MacIntyre, A. (1966). *A short history of ethics.* New York, NY: Macmillan.

MacIntyre, A. (1984). *After virtue* (2nd ed.). Notre Dame, IN: University of Notre Dame.

Maher, F. (2001). John Dewey, progressive education, and feminist pedagogies: Issues in gender and authority. In K. Weiler (Ed.), *Feminist engagements: Reading, resisting, and revisioning male theorists in education and cultural studies* (pp. 13–32). New York, NY: Routledge.

Marshall, C. (1997). Dismantling and reconstructing policy analysis. In C. Marshall (Ed.), *Feminist critical policy analysis* (Vol. 1). London, UK: Falmer.

Marshall, C., & Oliva, M. (Eds.). (2010). *Leadership for social justice: Making revolutions in education* (2nd ed.). Boston, MA: Allyn & Bacon.

Maslow, A. (1987). *Motivation and personality* (3rd ed.). New York, NY: Addison-Wesley.

Maxcy, S. J. (2002). *Ethical school leadership.* Lanham, MD: Scarecrow.

McCarthy, M. M. (1999). The evolution of educational leadership preparation programs. In J. Murphy & K. Seashore-Louis (Eds.), *Handbook of research on educational administration* (2nd ed.). San Francisco, CA: Jossey-Bass.

McKenzie, K. B., Christman, D. E., Hernandez, F., Fierro, E., Capper, C. A., Dantley, M., . . . Scheurich, J. (2008). From the field: A proposal for educating leaders for social justice. *Educational Administration Quarterly, 44*(1), 111–138.

Mezirow, J. (Ed.). (2000). *Learning as transformation: Critical perspectives on a theory in progress.* San Francisco, CA: Jossey-Bass.

Midgley, M. (1991). The origins of ethics. In P. Singer (Ed.), *A companion to ethics* (pp. 3–13). Malden, MA: Blackwell.

Nafisi, A. (2005). Mysterious connections that link us together. Washington, DC: National Public Radio. Retrieved from http://www.npr.org/templates/story/story.php?storyId=4753976.

Nanji, A. (1991). Islamic ethics. In P. Singer (Ed.), *A companion to ethics* (pp. 106–118). Malden, MA: Blackwell.

National Policy Board for Educational Administration (NPBEA). (2011). Educational leadership program standards: 2011 ELCC building level. Retrieved from http://www.ncate.org/LinkClick.aspx?fileticket=zRZI73R0nOQ%3D&tabid=676.

Noddings, N. (1992). *The challenge to care in schools.* New York, NY: Teachers College, Columbia University.

Noddings, N. (1995). *Philosophy of Education.* Dimensions of Philosophy Series. Boulder, CO: Westview Press.

Noddings, N. (2003). *Caring: A feminine approach to ethics and moral education* (2nd ed.). New York, NY: Teachers College, Columbia University.

O'Neill, O. (1991). Kantian ethics. In P. Singer (Ed.), *A companion to ethics* (pp. 175–185). Malden, MA: Blackwell.

Palmer, P. J. (2004). *A hidden wholeness: The journey toward an undivided life.* San Francisco, CA: Jossey-Bass.

Pollack, T. (2012). The miseducation of a beginning teacher: One educator's critical reflections on the functions and power of deficit narratives. *Multicultural Perspectives, 14*(2), 93–98.

Pounder, D., Reitzug, U., & Young, M. D. (2002). Preparing school leaders for school improvement, social justice and community. In J. Murphy (Ed.), *The educational leadership challenge. Redefining leadership for the 21st century* (pp. 261–288). Chicago, IL: National Society for the Study of Education.

Radd, S. I. (2007). *Connecting private roads to public highways: Toward a theory of school leadership for social justice.* Available from ProQuest Dissertations and Theses Database. (AAT 3295792).

Rawls, J. (1971). *A theory of justice.* Cambridge, MA: Harvard University.

Riehl, C. (2000). The principal's role in creating inclusive schools for diverse students: A review of normative, empirical, and critical literature on the practice of educational administration. *Review of Educational Research, 70*(1), 55–81.

Roberto, M. A. (2005). *Why great leaders don't take yes for an answer: Managing for conflict and consensus.* Upper Saddle River, NJ: Wharton School.

Robinson, D., & Garratt, C. (2004). *Introducing ethics.* London, UK: Icon Books.

Rodriguez, G. M., & Fabrionar, J. O. (2010). The impact of poverty on students and schools: Exploring the social justice leadership implications. In C. Marshall & M. Oliva (Eds.), *Leadership for social justice: Making revolutions in education* (2nd ed., pp. 55–73). New York, NY: Pearson.

Rowe, C. (1991). Ethics in ancient Greece. In P. Singer (Ed.), *A companion to ethics* (pp. 121–132). Malden, MA: Blackwell.

Ruether, R. (1992). *Gaia and God: An ecofeminist theology of earth healing.* San Francisco, CA: Harper.

Rusch, E. (2004). Gender and race in leadership preparation: A constrained discourse. *Educational Administration Quarterly, 40*(1), 16–48.

Scheurich, J. J., & Skrla, L. (2003). *Leadership for equity and excellence.* Thousand Oaks, CA: Corwin.

Schneewind, J. B. (1991). Modern moral philosophy. In P. Singer (Ed.), *A companion to ethics* (pp. 147–157). Malden, MA: Blackwell.

Seigfried, C. H. (1996). *Pragmatism and feminism: Reweaving the social fabric.* Chicago, IL: University of Chicago.

Sergiovanni, T. J. (1992). *Moral leadership: Getting to the heart of school improvement.* San Francisco, CA: Jossey-Bass.

Sergiovanni, T. J. (1995). *The principalship: A reflective practice perspective.* San Francisco, CA: Jossey-Bass.

Shapiro, J. P., & Stefkovich, J. A. (2005). *Ethical leadership and decision making in education* (2nd ed.). Mahwah, NJ: Lawrence Erlbaum.

Skrla, L., Scheurich, J. J., Garcia, J., & Nolly, G. (2010). Equity audits: A practical leadership tool for developing equitable and excellent schools. In C. Marshall & M. Oliva (Eds.), *Leadership for social justice: Making revolutions in education* (2nd ed., pp. 259–283). New York, NY: Pearson.

Spring, J. (2001). *Globalization and educational rights: An intercivilizational analysis.* Mahwah, NJ: Lawrence Erlbaum.

Starratt, R. J. (1994). *Building the ethical school.* New York, NY: Falmer.

Starratt, R. J. (1996). *Transforming educational administration: Meaning, community and excellence.* New York, NY: McGraw-Hill.

Starratt, R. J. (2003). *Centering educational administration: Cultivating meaning, community, responsibility.* Mahwah, NJ: Lawrence Erlbaum.

Starratt, R. J. (2004). *Ethical leadership.* San Francisco, CA: Jossey-Bass.

Strike, K. (2006). *Ethical leadership in schools: Creating community in an environment of accountability.* Thousand Oaks, CA: Corwin.

Strike, K. A., Haller, E. J., & Soltis, J. F. (1998). *The ethics of school administration* (2nd ed.). New York, NY: Teachers College.

Tannen, D. (1999). *The argument culture: Moving from debate to dialogue*. New York, NY: Random House.

Theoharis, G. (2007). Social justice educational leaders and resistance. Toward a theory of social justice leadership. *Educational Administration Quarterly, 43*(2), 221–258.

Thompson, M. (2003). *Ethics*. London, UK: Hodder Headline.

Vaill, P. B. (1996). *Learning as a way of being: Strategies for survival in a world of permanent white water*. San Francisco, CA: Jossey-Bass.

Van Cleave, M. (1994). *The least of these: Stories of schoolchildren*. Thousand Oaks, CA: Corwin.

Walker, K. L. (2010). Deficit thinking and the effective teacher. *Education and Urban Society, 43*, 576. doi:10.1177/001312451038072.

Walker, M. U. (1998). *Moral understandings: A feminist study in ethics*. New York, NY: Routledge.

Index